thank you FOR YOUR UNSOLICITED PARENTING ADVICE

ANDREA HOLMAN

Unless otherwise noted all Scripture taken from The Holy Bible, English Standard Version. ESV® Text Edition: 2016. Copyright © 2001 by Crossway Bibles, a publishing ministry of Good News Publishers.

Also used: the Holy Bible, New International Version®, NIV® Copyright ©1973, 1978, 1984, 2011 by Biblica, Inc.® Used by permission. All rights reserved worldwide.

Also used: the New King James Version®. Copyright © 1982 by Thomas Nelson. Used by permission. All rights reserved.

Copyright © 2025 Andrea Holman

All rights reserved. No part of this publication may be reproduced or transmitted in any form or by any means, electronic or mechanical, including photocopy, recording, or any information storage and retrieval system, without permission in writing from the publisher.

Printed in the United States.

ISBN 978-1-7371610-2-8 Paperback
ISBN 978-1-7371610-3-5 Hardcover
ISBN 978-1-7371610-4-2 Ebook

CONTENTS

CHAPTER ONE: Pregnancy Should Come with a Warning Label . . . 1

CHAPTER TWO: Understanding the Source and the Motive 25

CHAPTER THREE: External Influences 45

CHAPTER FOUR: Evaluating the Advice 75

CHAPTER FIVE: Responding to Unsolicited Advice 91

CHAPTER SIX:
Dealing with Persistent Unsolicited Parenting Advice 111

CHAPTER SEVEN: Seeking Advice 135

CHAPTER EIGHT:
Learning Is a Process and Mistakes are Inevitable 159

CHAPTER NINE: Prioritizing the Needs of Your Family 183

CHAPTER TEN: The Mantle We Leave Behind 205

CHAPTER ELEVEN: Embracing the Beautiful Unknown 227

Endnotes 245

About the Author 247

CHAPTER ONE

PREGNANCY SHOULD COME WITH A WARNING LABEL

I will praise You, for I am fearfully and wonderfully made;
Marvelous are Your works, and that my soul knows very well.

—Psalm 139:14 NKJV

Finding out you're pregnant might just be the grand entry into a club you never signed up for—the sort of club where the members, bless their hearts, don't wait for an invitation to share a piece of their mind. It's a community of moms who've walked the path, those trudging it right now, and others who daydream about the journey.

Once you're sporting a baby bump, it's like you're wearing a sign that says, "Open for Advice." Suddenly, every grocery store aisle or park bench can turn into an unscheduled seminar on baby-rearing. A stranger might just saunter over, give your belly an affectionate pat (yes, without asking!), and launch into tales and tips that you didn't request.

Sometimes, it's downright sweet. Like getting handed down creative twists for your baby's scrapbook or learning about the best deals on cribs that won't fall apart on you. But then, there are the times that'll have you stepping back, wondering if personal space just up and vanished. Like when a well-meaning soul dives into the details of breastfeeding challenges complete with remedies involving—get this—frozen lettuce leaves tucked into your bra.

Yes, dear, it's a real suggestion out there in the wild world of mothering advice. It's a thing!

So, what's this book about, you ask? Well, it's not about the icy vegetable fashion statement but rather the wild, wacky universe of unsolicited parenting advice that you'll wade through from here on out. And how to not just get by but really thrive among the chaos of dos and don'ts tossed your way.

Now, here's a little tidbit from me (and since you're holding this book, I'll assume I'm not overstepping): Treat advice like a buffet. There's plenty laid out in front of you—pick what suits your taste, what nourishes your soul, and if anything smells fishy, girl, well just walk on by.

You've been duly warned—and welcome to parenthood!

My Initiation to the Club

Have you ever found yourself inadvertently asking for advice? It might not dawn on you right at the moment, but the minute you share a trouble or two, brace yourself for an incoming flood of supposed solutions. Heck, isn't that why we share our troubles in the first place? To fish for a little guidance? Or at least that's what some folks seem to think.

Now, I've received some downright exasperating advice over the years, often when I've shared my heaviest burdens or even during those vulnerable moments when I ask for prayers. My momma used to caution me, "Honey, be careful who you tell your prayer requests to—you never know who's praying for or against you." I didn't quite catch her drift until I became a prayer-warrior mom myself. Goodness! Someone out there must be praying for my patience because it seems like it's always being put through the wringer!

And then there's my sister. I love that woman to bits, but Lord have mercy, sisters have a way of saying things no one else would dare. She has the uncanny ability to yank the rug right out from under me and plunk me straight down on the firm ground of reality. And she did just that to me not too long ago. Let me paint you a picture of that day.

It was a tough time; I'd just gotten some heart-wrenching news from the doctor about one of my little ones. (Which, by the way, some of mine are full-blown adults these days, but they'll always be my little ones, am I right?) As I spilled my fears and frustrations to her over the phone, pouring out my soul about the doctor's recommendations and the unsolicited advice from others, she just listened. I was a mess, grappling with the whys and the what-fors of our situation.

After what felt like an eternity of my rambling and a brief pause to catch my breath, my sister took a slow, deliberate breath and dropped a bombshell. In the calmest tone you can imagine, she said, "Have you considered that maybe, just maybe, this isn't all about you or your child?"

Well, I nearly dropped the phone. "You shut your face!" I snapped back. "I don't like you anymore!" In that moment, I wanted nothing more than to reach through that phone and give her a piece of my mind.

As much as it stung, deep down, I knew she was right. What we were going through might very well serve as a lesson for someone else watching how we handled these trials. But right then? I didn't want raw truth; I wanted comfort and a shoulder to cry on, not a slap of reality.

Despite my heated demand for her to "shut her face," which she outright ignored, my sister showed me a hard truth. We can't open up our lives to those we love and then get all bent out of shape when they serve back some hard-to-swallow truths. Not everyone can dish out such straightforward advice, but we all have someone in our lives who doesn't shy away from giving it to us straight. We value them, respect their courage, and trust their words because they're deeply invested in our well-being—even when their truths hit us like a ton of bricks.

It's tough to hear, tougher still to accept, and it rattles you right down to your emotional core. That's why it's critical to sift through all the parenting advice thrown your way. My sister calls these reality checks "tough love." I prefer to think of them as "Unsolicited Parenting Advice," delivered straight from the heart, with no sugarcoating in sight.

Unsolicited parenting advice is one of those inevitable parts of life that's as free as the air we breathe, especially when you're wearing the "new mom" badge. It doesn't matter where you're at—be it line-dancing at the grocery store, elbow-deep in work, praising high at church, or shopping for a family-size minivan—if it's even whispered that you've got a bun in the oven or are trying to start a family, well, honey, that's like sending up a signal flare for every baby whisperer in the vicinity to come running with a heap of advice.

Take me, for instance. When I was expecting our firstborn, I couldn't gain weight to save my life—or so it seemed. Now, hold off on thinking this was some vanity-inspired miracle. My situation was due to a relentless bout of morning sickness. I tried every trick in the book, but nothing stayed down. Naturally, this was more than a little worrying. If I couldn't nourish myself, how in the world was I supposed to nourish my little one? Was my body really the safe haven it needed to be for him?

Then, there was that unforgettable day when a well-meaning coworker suggested maybe I wasn't eating enough in an effort to keep my figure sleek. This—while I was navigating a sea of nausea. Seems she thought she was helping when she recommended I keep a food log. That was about the last straw. I retorted, a bit sharper than intended, "Darlin', it's a simple choice for me every day. I can either starve or stick to the few things that don't torture me twice—going down and coming back up. I'm familiar enough with what I eat, seeing as I meet it twice, so no, I won't be jotting it down."

Such encounters are par for the course when you're a mom-to-be, it seems. It's a crash course in biting your tongue and sometimes, just sometimes, reminding folks that while advice is as plentiful as potluck at a picnic, not every dish served is to your taste.

Expect the Unexpected Advice

Now, mommas, I could fill a book—or three—with the wild and whimsical advice that comes your way once you let slip that you're thinking about having a baby. It's as if announcing your plans to start a family flips a switch in folks, and suddenly, everyone's an expert in fertility.

From the moment you hint at wanting little footprints around your home, the floodgates open. You'll be introduced to a slew of should-dos and must-tries that never made it into those health class lectures. "Honey, if you're aiming to get pregnant, remember—gravity's your best friend after intimacy. Prop up those pillows, lie back, and think of England . . . or whatever floats your boat."

And the advice doesn't stop at conception. Oh no, it follows you down every grocery aisle. Like the time an elderly lady, bless her heart, handed me her recommended reading on ancient Chinese wisdom, including graphic illustrations that'd make a seasoned gynecologist blush. Caught off-guard while reaching for my bananas, I made a beeline for the checkout.

Once you've got a bun in the oven, well, that's when everyone has something to say about what you're eating, how you're sitting, and whether you should be dyeing your hair. "Sweetie, drop that sushi right now," or "Make sure you're eating enough for two," they say. And, "Watch that weight, darling, or you'll be wrestling with it long after the baby's born!" As if a pregnant gal needs to hear that. And which is it? Eat for two or watch your weight? One momma can't do it all!

Labor and delivery tips? Oh, they come in droves. You'll find yourself caught between the natural birth advocates who tout the glory of quick recoveries and the serene wisdom of those who've embraced the epidural. "Child, God didn't make us suffer more than necessary. Embrace the wonders of medicine!" Then there's the other camp, armed with tales of empowerment and minimal intervention. "Go natural, sweetheart. It's better for you and the baby!"

But it's the stories that start sweet and take a nosedive into horror that really test your mettle. One minute, you're chatting about effective labor positions, and the next, someone's sharing a graphic tale of tears and stitches that could turn your hair white.

Despite the avalanche of unsolicited wisdom, I keep my own labor tales close to my chest for the sake of this book. Some stories are better left unshared, though I'll let you in on a little secret: Never underestimate the power of a good pedicure. When those labor pains hit, at least you can look down and think, "Well, aren't my toes just the prettiest?" That's something, right?

So, buckle up, buttercup. You're in for a ride filled with more advice than you can shake a stick at. But remember, just like at a potluck, you don't have to try everything on the table. Pick what suits you, leave what doesn't, and above all, keep your sense of humor handy. You're gonna need it.

Navigating the Tides of Non-Traditional Parenthood

Becoming a mother comes in many beautiful and varied forms beyond the traditional husband and wife having a biological baby—adoption, in vitro fertilization, surrogacy, and through blending families. Each path holds its unique joys and challenges, and yet, somehow, unsolicited advice seems to be a universal experience across them all. Take my dear friend, for example, who navigated the complex waters of adopting a bi-racial child. The number of uninvited questions she faced could overwhelm any saint. But she handles it all with a grace that makes ballet look clumsy—though, on occasion, she's had to set some overly nosy folks straight with the type of firm kindness that would earn a standing ovation.

Watching her tactfully shut down prying questions—reminding people that some queries are out of bounds and that not every question deserves an answer—is nothing short of awe-inspiring. I often joke that I'd pay good money for front-row seats to her masterclass in boundary-setting. Her adeptness in these interactions is a testament to the strength and resilience so many women find as they forge their paths in motherhood.

No matter how we step into the role of mom, it's undoubtedly one of the most formidable, unpredictable, yet utterly rewarding adventures we'll ever undertake. The stages of parenting stretch out with their unique sets of joys and trials, continually testing our limits and patience in ways we never imagined. And let's be honest—sometimes, the transformation within us is so profound it catches us off guard. But it's this very metamorphosis, with all its trials and triumphs, that carves out the depth of our love and commitment.

Amid the daily grind, those moments of pure joy might slip unnoticed, but they are always there. One day, you're gently braiding your little girl's hair, focusing on every twist and turn, and the next, she's asserting her independence, wanting to style her own hair for soccer practice. These transitions, subtle yet poignant, mark the fleeting nature of childhood.

Every mother's journey through these swift-growing years is unique, but a common thread binds us: the astonishment at how swiftly the time passes. A fellow mom once shared with me during a heart-to-heart, "One day, you're hugging them tight, and the next, you set them down, not realizing it's the last time you'll ever lift them up." And before you know it, they're packing for college, leaving you to wonder if you remembered to teach them to pack their underwear—or, more importantly, if you've prepared them enough for the world.

These reflections on motherhood, filled with laughter, love, and the occasional tear, are what build our legacy as mothers. They're the stories we pass down, the lessons we teach, and the love we share that lights the path for generations to come.

As we've come to identify, becoming a mom is where advice flows as freely as coffee at a diner, and y'all, it seems everyone's got a brew to share. Now, I've navigated through enough advice to fill a small library, and it seems the older your kids get, the more everyone has an opinion—because suddenly, the stakes feel like they're sky-high.

Starting with the basics, breastfeeding always lights up the advice scoreboard. You'll hear it all: "It's healthier to breastfeed, darling, just maybe not at the picnic!" Or, "Breastfeeding's as natural as breathing. Do it whenever, wherever. Those bothered can just deal with it." And then there's the real kicker that always gets me chuckling, "I opted for bottles because, frankly, being treated like a dairy farm wasn't my cup of tea. Besides, once they get teeth, you'll wish you'd done the same!"

Then there's the downright bizarre, like the tip I got about chilling lettuce leaves and using them for nursing relief. Yes, like I said—lettuce! Trust me, nothing prepares you for stashing veggies in your lingerie!

Now, let's talk about bonding and balancing this circus called life. Some say, "Put that baby down before you spoil 'em. They need to learn to self-soothe!" Then, in the next breath, someone else is all, "Why not sleep with your baby? Maximize that bonding time." My favorite? "Sure, we bond all day, but this momma needs her beauty sleep—and maybe even a shower long enough to remember my own name."

Work-life balance? Oh, that's a good one. "If you love that baby, shouldn't you stay home?" And on the flip side, "Aren't you eager to get back to work? Babies need their social circles too!" And the timeless, "Sleep when the baby sleeps. Let the housework pile up!" Great in theory, but who's volunteering to come over and tackle Mount Laundry?

Of course, everyone insists you soak up every precious moment. "Put down that phone and just be present!" they say. But let's be real: If it weren't for those phones, half of our kids' antics wouldn't be documented for posterity—or for laughs when we're old and gray.

And don't forget the all-important self-care sermons. "Take time for yourself, it's crucial." Sounds lovely, but finding that time? Might as well schedule it between a mythical nap and a unicorn sighting.

But mommas, it's not just the tips; it's the things they don't warn you about that'll send you reeling. Like, who knew that a toddler's grip could rival a crocodile's? Or that "pull here" on a fire alarm isn't an invitation for a curious preschooler? Trust me, learning that the hard way makes for a memorable parent-teacher conference.

Through every unsolicited piece of advice and every well-meaning but sometimes misguided comment, the journey of motherhood is a wild ride, made all the richer by these shared experiences. So whether you take the advice with a grain of salt or a whole salt shaker, remember this: In motherhood, we're all in this together, navigating the highs, the lows, and the absurdities with a little help from our friends, a lot of laughter, and an endless supply of love.

And, just as you think you've got a handle on this whole parenting gig, the day comes that'll squeeze your heart more than any other—the day they head off to college. You thought the toddler years were tough? College is a whole different ball game, with a fresh batch of advice and concerns that'll have you wishing for the simpler days of "lettuce leaves" and diaper disasters. I remember chuckling nervously as we talked through every imaginable scenario with our son before he left for college. We covered everything from study habits to managing freedom, and as a parting gift, we even snagged an air filter for his dorm room because, let's face it, teenage boys and freshness don't always go hand in hand.

And let me tell you about coping mechanisms—after we dropped off each of our first two boys at their dorms, my house felt eerily quiet, like someone turned off the very soundtrack of my life. That's when I found comfort in the pitter-patter of new, furry feet. Hershey and Oreo, two pups as sweet as their names suggest, came into our lives and filled that empty nest with joy and a bit of playful chaos. Pets, I found, do wonders for separation anxiety (mine, not theirs).

Throughout these transitions, the advice never stops coming. It seems like everyone has the perfect blueprint for navigating college years. And as they doled out their pearls of wisdom, I often found myself biting my tongue, thinking, "Really? I thought by now I'd have earned some credibility in this parenting role!" But no, the unsolicited guidance flows as freely as ever.

Through all the unwarranted pieces of advice, I've gleaned a couple of hard-earned truths that have become my north star. First, I've realized I'll never quite match up to everyone's lofty parenting ideals—and that's perfectly okay. More importantly, I've embraced the liberating fact that the only opinions that truly matter in shaping our children's lives are those of my husband and me—and, most critically, the guiding light we receive from above. It's a freeing thought, knowing that at the end of the day, we answer to our own consciences and the values we hold dear, not the chorus of well-meaners.

As you journey through your own parenting chapters, from the baby steps to the big leaps, remember these lessons. They're not just about surviving the advice onslaught but thriving in the truth that you are the best parent for your child—equipped uniquely by your experiences and your faith. Let that confidence anchor you as you and your partner steer your family ship, guided by the stars of your shared values and convictions.

How Unsolicited Advice Affects Emotional and Mental Health

Let's dive into the tangled web of unsolicited advice and its impact on both our emotional and mental health. It's important to start by clarifying the distinction between these two closely linked aspects of our well-being. Emotional health centers on our feelings—how we navigate both the highs and the lows of our daily lives. Dr. Robert Rich, Jr., a respected medical director from North Carolina, once explained, "Being emotionally healthy doesn't mean you're happy all the time. It means you're aware of your emotions. You can deal with them, whether they're positive or negative."[1]

This distinction resonates deeply with me. Growing up, I felt the weight of expectations and often struggled to manage my emotions in a healthy way, especially when bombarded with advice that seemed to measure my worth against others. It's a journey to learn the right responses to these emotional tugs without landing yourself in hot water.

Mental health, on the other hand, relates to our thought processes—how we think, reason, and understand the world and our experiences within it. The Centers for Disease Control (CDC) describes mental health as encompassing our emotional, psychological, and social well-being.[2] These aspects of health are intertwined; our emotions color our thoughts, and our thoughts can stir our emotions, creating a complex dance that sometimes leaves us struggling to know which step came first.

Physical conditions can complicate this dance even further. Dr. Rich points out that mental health issues can have both emotional and physical causes, including genetics or hormonal imbalances, and external pressures from work, family, or school can exacerbate these issues. He notes that stress, combined with isolation or feeling overwhelmed, can significantly affect our mental well-being.

To sum it up:
- Emotional health is about managing how we feel.
- Mental health is about managing how we think.
- Challenges in one area can influence and complicate the other.

Emotional and mental health are fundamental to navigating life, and that includes handling the curveballs of parenting. From the hormonal rollercoasters to the sleepless nights, parenting—even under the best circumstances—can test the sturdiest of us. And here's where unsolicited advice often comes into play, adding an extra layer of stress.

We frequently receive parenting advice that, although well-intentioned, can feel like a subtle critique of our choices. This can trigger a cascade of negative thoughts—like thinking a comment on breastfeeding is a direct attack on our capabilities as a mother. "They must think I'm a bad mom," or "What kind of mother can't nourish her child properly?" Such thoughts can spiral, impacting our emotional and mental health.

Moreover, sometimes, the advice comes with less than pure intentions—perhaps from those who feel a need to assert control or flaunt their perceived superiority. This not only stirs negative emotions but can also skew our perception of ourselves and our parenting.

However, as Dr. Rich aptly notes, recognizing when you need help is not a sign of weakness but a critical aspect of managing your emotional health. It's not a matter of if you'll need help, but when. Acknowledging this need can empower us to seek the right support, ensuring we remain strong, capable guardians for our little ones.

Amidst the whirlwind of motherhood and the barrage of unsolicited advice, remember this: Your journey is unique, and no one knows your child better than you do. While advice can sometimes help, trust your instincts and lean on your experience, enriched by genuine support from those who truly have your and your child's best interests at heart.

Don't be surprised if this sounds all too familiar—a natural response to the barrage of suggestions flung at any new mom who's been weathering more changes since her pregnancy kicked off than many weather in a lifetime. I've been right there in those boots, reacting just as strongly to well-meaning but sometimes overwhelming advice. Over time, though, this endless wellspring of parenting tips can really start to weigh on us. Every day, we're making countless decisions for ourselves and our little ones, most so routine they barely make a blip on our daily radar. We breeze through these choices, but seldom does anyone cheer on these quiet victories. But let a misstep happen? Oh, you bet there's a lineup ready to offer their two cents, eager to critique at the first slip-up.

When we start letting unsolicited advice chip away at us, doubting every diaper change and dinner choice, insecurity starts to gnaw at our confidence. Slowly but surely, what little peace we had starts to scatter to the winds, and the stress begins to gnaw not just at our minds but at our bodies too.

Despite the rosy pictures painted on social media, nobody's living that perfect scenario every day. We're all grappling with the anxieties and trials of parenthood. Feeling overwhelmed isn't a sign you're doing it wrong; it's par for the course in this job.

Being a mom is arguably the most emotionally taxing gig on the planet. We pour out love without condition, we sacrifice for their smiles, we push to be better today than we were yesterday—and all for what? For the chaotic mix of stress, sticky fingerprints, slobbery kisses, and the occasional sass. And why? Because the immense love for those little hearts steals ours every single day.

We all catch ourselves daydreaming about those picture-perfect family snapshots, wondering what it might be like to step into that seemingly flawless life, even just for a day. When you find yourself yearning for a glimpse into someone else's world, remember—your feelings are valid, but they don't always paint the full picture. Behind every "perfect" scene are unseen struggles.

So, regardless of the advice hurled your way or how often you feel pressed to match up to someone else's highlight reel, remember: Your path is uniquely yours. The decisions you make are shaped by a tapestry of influences—your background, beliefs, health, and the life experiences you carry with you.

No two parenting journeys are identical, even if the milestones look similar. While family, friends, and even strangers in the parenting sphere might offer their insights, remember, this story is yours—intimately personal and uniquely beautiful.

Cameron's Story

One of my earliest lessons as a mom was a stark reminder that despite all the advice you gather trying to script the perfect birth story for your child, God's plans are often written quite differently.

I meticulously followed every doctor's order and weighed all the well-meaning advice. Still, despite my best efforts, I found myself on bed rest and unexpectedly went into preterm labor at thirty-five weeks. My little one was all set for a dramatic early entrance!

The day only grew more chaotic as I arrived at the emergency room during a blizzard under a full moon. The hospital was unusually bustling with three sets of twins all lined up for C-sections, and there I was, in a hospital with only two operating rooms available.

As the hours ticked by, fraught with attempts to deliver naturally, it became clear that my baby boy wouldn't make his entry into the world without further intervention. That evening, it was determined I needed an emergency C-section for both our sakes, but there were no rooms ready and not enough doctors on hand. When we finally got into an operating room, the baby monitor indicated my son was in distress, and my overwhelming fear of surgery loomed large over me. My mind was a whirlwind of doubts and questions. Had I missed something? Was there something wrong with me? Why couldn't my body just do what it was supposed to do? I had done everything right—from strict bed rest to religiously following medical advice.

But then, as I was prepped on the operating table, everything shifted. The room fell eerily silent as the baby monitor stopped, and the doctor's urgent command to "Get him out now!" echoed through the room. Those ninety seconds—the longest and most terrifying of my life—felt like an eternity until, finally, my son was brought into the world. He was born silent and blue, with the cord wrapped twice around his neck. After some tense moments, he took his first gentle breath—his first victory in this big world.

That harrowing experience of facing my profound fear of surgery—my second-greatest fear—ironically turned out to be the very thing that saved my son's life. The flood of emotions and the trauma that came with it were immense—a whirlwind that took a long time for a new mom to process. But through it all, it was a poignant reminder that life's script doesn't always follow our meticulously laid plans.

That day in the blizzard, as my son Cameron made his early entrance into the world, it became crystal clear that we were just players in a story God had already penned. Despite all the precautions and the medical interventions aimed at dodging complications and avoiding a C-section, it turned out that very procedure saved Cameron's life. Had we evaded preterm labor or skirted around the necessity for a C-section, my boy might've been in that precarious position, his cord wrapped tightly around his neck, for far too long. In the chaos of that stormy night, with twins being delivered left and right, what seemed like a catastrophe was actually a divine gift. The hands needed to save my son were right there, prepared by God's impeccable timing.

By fifteen months old, Cameron was diagnosed with cerebral palsy, stemming from those tense moments lacking oxygen at birth. All four of my children were brought into this world via C-section, each of them facing their unique battles. With each diagnosis, I wrestled with guilt, feeling like a failure as a mother, and yes, I even harbored some anger toward God. Why my children? Why such heavy burdens for such little shoulders?

Here's where perception shifts. The journey of motherhood, intertwined with these challenges, has been an unexpected gift, unveiling profound lessons and blessings along the way. But recognizing these gifts didn't come easy or quickly—it took time, growth, and experience to truly see and appreciate them.

That tough conversation with my sister happened during another one of my children's medical diagnoses. I was in pieces, searching for some semblance of meaning, when I blurted out for her to "shut her face." What she said next stopped me cold: "Every moment that touches your life isn't always for you. Sometimes, it's for those watching. You might see the impact, or you might never understand why—but you have to be okay with that and trust God through even the horrible parts."

Motherhood is a series of life-and-death decisions. We pore over research, take advice from doctors, listen to those we trust, and use our best judgment. And through it all, God holds the reins.

From his moment of conception and in every breath he takes, God's hand has been on Cameron's life. Every moment of that frigid, tempestuous night and each day since was orchestrated by a greater plan—one that I couldn't see or understand as I lay on that operating table. That night, amidst my greatest fears, God was not just saving my son; He was also shaping me into the mother Cameron needed—tailored by divine design for the challenges ahead.

Despite my faith in a higher purpose, the burden of believing I had failed my son because of my body's shortcomings weighed heavily on me. It clouded my emotional and mental well-being, focusing my heart on what went wrong instead of the miracles unfolding. It took time, but I eventually recognized that even in those moments of perceived failure, God was at work. He was crafting a path that only I could walk with Cameron, one that no one else could tread.

We often wish we could rewrite parts of our stories, erase the painful bits, or redo the tough chapters. But even if I had the power, I wouldn't erase that day. It's a part of our story that, while fraught with fear and pain, brought with it irreplaceable blessings and lessons. We don't always see God's plan in the moment, but I trust in His timing. It's always perfect, revealing just what we need when we need it. Now, I watch and wait, eager to see how God's plan for Cameron unfolds, grateful for every chapter that we get to experience together, no matter how challenging.

Be You

Some folks ask me how I manage with four kids, each with their significant needs. It's no walk in the park, I'll tell you that. But then, I hear stories from other moms, tales of trials that would surely have me down for the count, and I realize that God crafts each of us for our unique challenges. I'm certain of one thing: I can only be the truest version of myself. Trying to be anyone else is like a peach trying to be a plum—it's just not going to happen. My role? To be the best darn peach I can be while cheering on the plums to shine in their own right.

Each of us is uniquely equipped for our own paths, blessed with distinct gifts, talents, and experiences that shape not only our lives but also those around us. It's truly remarkable when a piece of advice profoundly impacts your family, bringing peace, clarity, and calm to your life. That's how you know it was meant for you. Remember, God scripts every journey—yours and mine—and no slew of advice can wrest His pen away. We're here to uplift each other, but remember, I can't play the role God has designed for you, and you can't take on mine. Embrace being you—there's no one better suited for your life's role than you.

Your mission is to embrace your unique self. God has instilled invaluable qualities in you that help nurture your children and guide them toward their purpose. Often, we question whether what we bring to the table as mothers is enough, but rest assured, you are precisely what your family needs. They deserve the real, whole you. So go ahead, and just do you!

Sister, if you find yourself worn down from the barrage of unsolicited parenting advice, it's time to let that burden slide off your shoulders. It's a well-established fact that the emotional weight of constant advice can be downright overwhelming. When those lying feelings threaten to shake your peace, it's crucial to cast them aside and refocus on your core values. I test everything against these values and rest in the steadfast grace and love God holds for my family throughout our journey.

Navigating the waters of unsolicited advice demands sharp discernment. My hope is that as we walk this path together, you'll feel not just supported but empowered. We'll develop strategies to sift through the advice, identify useful bits, and reinforce your confidence to trust your own instincts and unique parenting style. By the end, we'll also look at what we want to pass on to our kiddos as they find their place in this world.

Reflect on your journey—look back at who you were and recognize how much you've grown. You're doing wonderfully, momma! Seeing where you started and where you are now should give you the courage to take thoughtful steps forward.

So, come along on this adventure into the realm of unsolicited parenting advice. Let's journey toward self-discovery, resilience, and empowerment, aiming to foster a nurturing and loving environment for our children.

Above all, I urge you to remain true to yourself, not succumbing to the world's pressures. God crafted a unique mom in you, perfectly paired with your children, who fills your soul and tests your heart in equal measure. Together, we'll navigate this labyrinth, emerging stronger, wiser, and more assured in our roles as mothers.

REFLECTIONS

A Mother Like Me

Scripture Reading: Matthew 1:18-25

Have you ever thought about what it may have been like for Mary, the virgin mother of Jesus, when she learned she was pregnant with the Son of God? The news would have been a tremendous shock to anyone, let alone a betrothed teenage girl from the small town of Nazareth. Mary had a lot to process, including the implications of a divine, yet extra-marital, pregnancy and the challenges that would come with raising the Son of God.

Can you even imagine the unsolicited advice Mary may have received? Take a moment to stop and consider some of the comments she may have heard from family, friends, and strangers. At that time, a pre-marital pregnancy was so scandalous that Mary could have lost her reputation, her fiancée, and even her life. Furthermore, the announcement of a divine, immaculate conception to give birth to the long-awaited savior would lead to disbelief, ridicule, and judgment. Despite these potential challenges, Mary remained faithful and willing to accept the role God had chosen for her.

Just like Mary, you have also been specially chosen by God to carry your children. You play a very special and significant role in carrying, nurturing, caring for, and raising your children to the best of your ability and to the glory of God.

Your circumstances may not be as extraordinary as Mary's, but both you and your situation are unique. I encourage you to trust God's plan and embrace the faith He has in you, especially when you don't comply with someone else's definition of motherhood, go against the grain, or could even be considered a rebel.

Prayer

Heavenly Father,

Thank You for the sacred gift of motherhood, with all its joys, challenges, and unexpected moments. You have uniquely crafted each of us to nurture, guide, and love the children You've entrusted to our care. When the voices of unsolicited advice grow loud, help us to quiet our hearts and listen for Your still, small voice that speaks truth, wisdom, and peace.

Grant us discernment to sift through the noise, courage to stand firm in our convictions, and grace to respond with kindness, even when the words we hear sting. Like Mary, may we carry our roles with humility and strength, trusting in Your divine purpose even when the path feels uncertain. Remind us that we are fearfully and wonderfully made, chosen by You for such a time as this.

Fill our hearts with confidence, knowing that we are the perfect mothers for our children—not because we are perfect, but because You are. May we lead with love, rooted in faith, and may our children see Your reflection in the way we nurture, correct, and cherish them.

Thank You for walking with us through every season, holding us close when we feel overwhelmed, and rejoicing with us in every victory, big or small. Help us embrace the journey, trusting that You are the author of our stories, weaving beauty from even the most unexpected chapters.

In Jesus' name, Amen.

Small Group Discussion Questions

1. What has been your experience with unsolicited parenting advice? Share one memorable piece of advice and its impact on you.
2. Considering Mary's story, how can her faith and grace under pressure guide modern mothers facing judgment or criticism?
3. Have you ever felt emotionally affected by unsolicited parenting advice? Describe how you dealt with it.
4. Discuss a time when advice felt supportive versus when it felt undermining. How do you distinguish helpful from harmful advice?
5. How do you balance trusting your instincts with the abundance of parenting advice available?
6. How does your faith shape your parenting decisions? Share how your spiritual beliefs influence your approach to motherhood.

Self-Care Affirmations

- I trust my instincts and make parenting decisions that feel right for my family.
- My journey is unique, and I am exactly the mom my children need.
- I embrace the role God has given me with courage and grace.
- I filter advice, keeping only what serves my family's best interests.
- I am capable of managing both praise and criticism with a peaceful heart.
- Every day, I grow stronger and more confident in my motherhood journey.

CHAPTER TWO

UNDERSTANDING THE SOURCE AND THE MOTIVE

Advice often springs from a place of concern, love, or a desire to pass on wisdom. Yet, the overwhelming flood and conflicting nature of this advice can leave us doubting our own instincts and second-guessing our decisions as parents. Just because we've joined the ranks of motherhood doesn't mean we have to carry every piece of advice home without questioning its fit.

Understanding the reasons behind unsolicited advice can illuminate their intentions and help us handle these moments with more empathy and insight.

Being a mom is a profound journey filled with love, joy, and countless moments of wonder, but it also brings its fair share of challenges. One significant challenge is wading through the sea of unsolicited parenting advice. As a mom, you've likely experienced this firsthand—well-meaning folks from all corners offering their two cents on how you should raise your child. While some pearls of wisdom may be valuable, they might not always jive with your own beliefs and instincts.

There's one place you never want to find yourself as a mom, but despite your best efforts, every mother ends up there at some point. Where's that, you might ask? It's when you catch yourself parenting according to someone else's expectations. When this happens, it can feel like a defeat, maybe even a bit of a betrayal, but remember, darlin', you do have a choice!

Years ago, while sitting in a doctor's office waiting room with my son Austin—the inspiration for my first book, *I Quit the Family*—I learned this lesson deeply. In the next room, a sweet momma struggled with her children during her newborn's checkup. Her older boy got more and more worked up, hollering at the top of his lungs, "I want to leave! I'm hungry!" My whole body tensed up, a flood of memories from arguments with Austin washing over me. I heard her hushed pleas for quiet, which only egged him on to scream louder and more often, much to his mom's chagrin.

My heart ached for her because I'd been right there in those same shoes, knowing all too well the thoughts racing through her mind: "This is so embarrassing! Everyone must think I'm a hot mess and the worst mom ever! Why didn't I bring more snacks? Why can't he just behave?"

I wanted so badly to offer her a reassuring hug and say, "Honey, we've all been there. This too shall pass."

But I didn't.

Instead, I stayed glued to my chair, knuckles white as I clutched the seat, caught up in my own embarrassment, realizing how I had succumbed to pressures and judgments from folks I couldn't even see. In those moments, Austin and my other children bore the brunt of my frustrations, anxieties, and disappointment over my inability to control the chaos—even when no one was watching.

Austin was diagnosed with ADHD as a youngster, and he couldn't handle being in public for more than twenty minutes before he'd have a meltdown. In those heavy moments, under the weight of judgmental stares, I found myself parenting him based on the expectations of folks who didn't know his struggles or how hard he was trying to control his reactions. I, too, in my weariness and embarrassment, often overlooked how tough it was for him to make sense of the world around him and to fit into the tight mold of what society deems normal.

I looked at my son one day and said, "My goodness, I did that! I did that to you!"

Austin might have chuckled, but I found no humor in my actions or how I had caved to external pressures. My mind was haunted by replays of what I now considered my top ten worst momma moments. I had been short with my kids and raised my voice more times than I could count, leading to many restless nights for us all. How many times had I succumbed to scenarios just like this?

I confessed to Austin, "I'm glad you can find a way to laugh because, son, I sure can't! I'm so sorry!"

What stung me the most in this realization was knowing that I knew better. But, worn down by exhaustion, like that dear momma in the waiting room, I was burdened with the weight of other people's advice and expectations. As my journey as a mom progressed, I lost bits of who I was and the beliefs I held dear. Instead of being the mom my children truly needed or the mom I aspired to be, I had parented according to the playbook others handed me, and it weighed heavy on my heart.

Why did I cling to advice that didn't fit? It felt easier to align with societal norms. It seemed like everyone wanted to be helpful. But, truth be told, I was too tired to sift through which advice was relevant to my situation. All I wanted was for the advice to work and for the scrutinizing glares to vanish.

There's a poignant story from *The Seven Habits of Highly Effective People* by Stephen Covey, where a father lets his children run wild on a subway. When a passenger gently confronted him, the father revealed his wife had just passed away at the hospital. The passenger's annoyance quickly turned to empathy, offering help instead.[3]

Understandably, the children's behavior was a reaction to their grief—a perfectly normal response under such tragic circumstances. No one would expect them to act as if it were just another day, so the usual advice simply didn't apply.

This was true for my Austin too. People expected him to act a certain way, but given his ADHD, that wasn't feasible. His "normal" was different, and I should have parented him based on realistic expectations for a child with his challenges.

That day in the doctor's office, as I listened to the struggles of the mother next door, I realized that the constant stream of unsolicited parenting advice had only fueled my insecurities, distancing me from the mother I yearned to be. I wondered if she was still in there, somewhere beneath all the expectations I had let define me. What if I had allowed Austin more space to be his true self and guided him through his challenges based on what I valued as his mom instead of bending to fit others' molds? We reached a good place eventually, but the journey was far tougher because I let the wrong outside voices shape my parenting.

There's no one better at making us feel inadequate as a mom than ourselves. We're all too familiar with our own doubts, fears, disappointments, and the secrets we keep tucked away. Instead of confronting my insecurities, I let them take the wheel, soaking up every scrap of advice on how to be a better mom. The more advice I gathered, the shakier my confidence became, making it hard to just stand firm in the belief that I'd pull through and everything would eventually be all right. Carrying around that load of insecurities can wear a momma down, let me tell you.

That day in the doctor's office was a turning point for me. I made a decision right then and there that would change our path forward. I chose to shut down those nagging insecure thoughts so I could reconnect with the mom I was meant to be, focusing on forging a better path. I realized as long as I kept breathing, I could strive to be a better mother today than I was the day before.

It was time to roll up my sleeves and do some serious work. As I started to tackle the layers of my insecurities, I uncovered two key factors that shaped the advice I received: the motive behind it and who was giving it. I learned that by considering the source and their intentions, I could sift through what advice was applicable to me and what I could let slide off my back.

Sometimes, a mother's advice stems from a genuine desire to help or connect. Other times, let's just say, her motives might not be as pure, and they might downright stink. It's crucial to learn how to filter advice and understand its underlying intent. It's part of our nature to seek connections, even if those connections come with their own set of risks.

The Open Hearts

A person with an open heart doesn't have any agenda other than to help you. She genuinely cares and has your best interests at heart—whether it's to share wisdom, spare you from a tough lesson, or celebrate the joys of motherhood with you. They approach you with nothing but good intentions, but even so, it's wise to sift through the advice they offer.

A momma with an open heart might check if you're open to suggestions before diving in. She's the type who listens more than she speaks, and when she does offer advice, you know it's worth leaning in for. She'll check in on how you're adjusting and how you're feeling and may even offer to follow up or lend a hand. A true sign of an open heart is acceptance of you just as you are and an understanding that what works for one child might not work for another. She won't judge you based on your decisions but supports what's best for your family, offering help through each season of your journey.

God created us for relationships and community; we need each other to thrive. Think back to the pioneer days when new moms had to be warned about dangers lurking like snakes or poisonous berries by the river. Sharing such vital information was crucial for the safety of the entire community. Keeping such knowledge to oneself could have led to grave consequences, casting doubt on one's intentions.

Our deep-seated need for connection is also crucial for our emotional and mental health. Every woman longs for a tribe—a group of other women committed to supporting one another for the betterment of all their families.

Social media has become a vibrant conduit for meeting other moms facing similar challenges. It enables us to forge strong bonds by connecting with moms across the globe. Women you may never meet in person can significantly impact your life, broadening your understanding, extending your community, and offering the validation you need as you navigate the reality of motherhood against its idealized image.

It's particularly special when you connect with a local mom in a global or regional social media group. Getting to know each other online might even lead to meeting up for playdates or lunch. After all, if people can meet their spouses online, why not make a few lifelong friends along the way?

We often embrace advice from strangers online because we're naturally wired for connection. While many folks are sincere, their motivations might be more personal than they appear. For instance, if a mom advises you to buck conventional wisdom because "that's what worked for her," she might be seeking validation for her own parenting choices.

A momma who shares advice entangled with her emotional experiences might be grappling with her unresolved past. Years after navigating tough waters, many of us are still dealing with the aftermath, trying to find peace. We dispense advice because, deep down, we're striving to connect—to feel heard and affirmed—so we don't feel so isolated. I treasure this aspect of motherhood; as I've matured in handling advice, I've become adept at spotting these moments. I've learned to listen attentively, pose thoughtful questions, and encourage fellow moms to express and process their emotions. It's genuinely fulfilling when I can sift through these advice-laden exchanges, serving both as a recipient and a giver, which deepens my ties to my core values and my community.

Certainly, we should seek and offer support and encouragement to one another, but our inherent need for connection can present challenges. If we're not careful, we might let others' corrections and critiques of our parenting sway us until we no longer recognize the mother reflected back at us in the mirror. If you find yourself searching for the momma you aspire to be and coming up short, well, "Houston, we have a problem!"

The Dirty Diapers

When I discovered I was expecting, one of the highlights was picking out my very first diaper bag. Now, y'all might chuckle, but I bypassed those highfalutin designer purses for the crème de la crème of baby bags! I was all about showing off that I was a diaper-bag-toting, baby-loving momma. I aimed for the works—a bag decked out with nifty pockets and accessories, from a quick-access binky pouch to a key loop, a drink holder, and even a sprawling, fold-out changing pad to keep those germs at bay from my little one's bottom! And, if dreams had wings, I'd have snagged a portable wipe warmer to keep my baby's behind toasty.

That designer diaper bag was a marvel—it had it all! But as my brood grew and the bag's contents expanded, that stylish sack got heavier with each passing year. I figured I'd tote less around as the kiddos aged, but no siree! By the time I had four kiddos under ten, that chic bag had morphed into a do-it-all powerhouse—part purse, part laptop carrier, part toy box, and even a Nintendo DS haven, games and all!

Imagine me, a loaded-up dairy cow, tromping into Starbucks with my hefty bag thwacking my thigh at every step. With a baby on one hip and a toddler clinging to my arm, I'd holler at the other two to quit their street racing. Oh, how I prayed every Starbucks came with a drive-thru for a quick double-pump Frappuccino grab—'cause the risk of mixing up kids on the way out was real! Although it was easy to spot mine—they were the ones no one else dared claim! Ha!

After many a bruised thigh and sore shoulder, I swapped that fancy diaper bag for a plain black backpack with three practical zippers. It wasn't nearly as stylish, but it did the trick, healed my hip and shoulder, and allowed me to stand up straight once again. So, here's to choosing functionality over flair when it comes to toting around your little one's necessities.

No matter how stylish or plain, every diaper bag serves one true purpose: hauling your baby's messes. Whether you're a cloth-diapering eco-momma or a disposable-diaper user (no side-eyes here, darlin'), at day's end, that diaper bag's gonna reek of milk spills, spit-up rags, and that overripe banana you forgot from breakfast.

To dodge the stink, we toss out those messy diapers, right? But imagine for a second if we decided to tuck away those used diapers in the bag for later use. Seems outrageous, doesn't it? Yet, if we learned anything from post-COVID shortages—yes, even those of diapers—it's the art of scrimping. But here's where I draw the line: reusing a disposable diaper is just not in the cards, no matter how thrifty we get!

Just like a soiled diaper, some folks' motives can stink to high heaven, leaving a sour trace that lingers. When advice is drenched in control, judgment, or any unsavory intent, it's time to chuck it faster than a dirty nappy and not give it a second glance. Hauling around such advice is like lugging a bag full of those ripe diapers—it chafes, weighs you down, and bends your spirit until standing straight feels like a daydream.

I've never pocketed a used diaper for a second round, and I encourage that some advice ought to hit the trash just as swiftly. Sometimes, you catch that foul stench right off the bat; other times, it takes a hot minute to sniff out where it's coming from. But let me tell you, when you do, it's best to toss it out and not pick it up again.

When you're drowning in a sea of advice, consider the source. God places specific folks in our lives, each meant to play their part, and the weight of their words often depends on the depth of our bond with them. Not every piece of advice will fit your life's puzzle, and that's all right. Know who's speaking into your life and why; determine the ones whose words may truly matter and will help you navigate through.

Each God-given person in our lives is there for a distinct purpose, and the dynamics of these relationships deeply influence the relevance and impact of the advice we receive.

Your Social Bedrock

Ever wondered about your social bedrock? Well, a bedrock is a foundation—it's essentially the fundamental principles and beliefs that you've built your life upon. Your social bedrock includes the people who help you build on that foundation. For many of us, our families form the core of this bedrock, shaping the values we cherish and aim to pass down through generations.

This bedrock includes the people who profoundly influence us—our inner circle. These folks, be they close friends or family, are deeply woven into the fabric of our lives. They offer advice from a place of love and genuine concern, aiming to bolster us, share family wisdom, and keep traditions alive.

As you navigate motherhood, you'll meet new versions of yourself, but your core—your bedrock—remains unshaken. It's what keeps you steady. When this core feels threatened or if advice starts to undermine it, that's when unrest stirs within us. We might feel obliged to heed the words of those we hold dear, but it's vital to sift this advice through the filter of our bedrock values.

Flexibility in handling advice is important, but so is balance. Protecting your values and peace of mind is paramount. If someone persists with advice that clashes with your principles, creating some space might be necessary. Remember, it's perfectly okay to politely decline advice and maintain the boundaries that safeguard what's best for your family.

If our inner circle is our bedrock, why do we sometimes feel compelled to seek validation from acquaintances or even strangers? This drive stems from our innate desire to connect and build relationships. But remember, not all relationships are created equal, and some can influence our family life more significantly than others.

Building relationships should be a deliberate process. We must gauge new connections against the principles we cherish, not the shifting sands of external expectations. We must remain steadfast, especially during challenging times, so that we stay true to our authentic selves. There's no need to rush; carefully weigh new ideas and relationships against your foundational values to see if they truly merit inclusion in your life.

Often, the most meaningful relationships need time and nurturing to reach their full potential. Stand firm in your values, and don't bend to external pressures that don't align with what's right for your family. By doing so, you ensure that your social circle supports and enriches your life rather than detracting from it.

Friends and Acquaintances

In your journey as a momma, you'll meet a wide array of friends and acquaintances from various walks of life—be it church, work, school, or other community circles. These folks often have a limited but genuine interest in your well-being, offering encouragement, sharing their own parenting tales, or imparting cultural or generational nuggets of wisdom.

While their intentions are usually good, their advice often comes from their own perspectives and experiences, which might not fully align with yours. They don't have the full story of your life and might miss key details that affect the relevance of their suggestions. That's precisely why it's necessary to establish strong boundaries. You need to be able to say, "Hold up now. Just because that works for you doesn't mean it's gonna suit my little ones."

Be clear about your own values and use them as a sieve for all the advice that comes your way. This discernment allows you to trust your gut when something doesn't quite sit right. Filtering advice through your values helps you make informed decisions that truly resonate with your family's needs. This way, you can step forward confidently, knowing that, no matter the outcome, you made the best choice for your family based on what you hold dear.

Strangers

Strangers often drift into your life for just a fleeting moment. They might be the sweetest souls you'll ever meet, but remember, they only catch a snapshot of your life, influenced solely by their own experiences. A stranger doesn't really have a stake in your day-to-day, and their insights are limited to what you reveal in brief encounters or what they observe in passing. Their motivations can vary widely—maybe they're just trying to be helpful based on their own life lessons, maybe they love to chat and meet new folks, or perhaps they just can't help but share their two cents, whether it's called for or not. Sometimes, though, a stranger might just say exactly what you need to hear, shaking your world with an unexpected truth.

For instance, a friend of mine, barely five feet tall, was showing a pretty big baby belly by five months pregnant. One day, a stranger in the elevator assumed she was expecting twins and insisted she get a second medical opinion. My friend, worn out and queasy, retorted sharply, "I'm having one girl, confirmed by four ultrasounds. I trust my doctor—he's been with me for years. You're off your rocker!"

Now, my friend didn't know this person from Adam and certainly didn't ask for a medical consultation right there in the elevator. The stranger's approach was intrusive, and honestly, both ladies could've handled the situation a bit more gracefully, especially considering they might bump into each other again!

But imagine if my friend dwelled on that encounter. What if she started second-guessing her doctor because of a comment from someone she'll never see again? "What if she's right? Is my doctor incompetent? Could I really be having twins? Should I have looked for a different doctor?" This kind of spiraling is exactly how a simple comment from a stranger can turn into a storm of doubt.

Unsolicited advice from strangers can burrow into our minds and stir up unnecessary worry. Why should we give such power to the words of someone who barely knows us? Thankfully, we don't have to. We have the choice to listen, assess, and then either take it to heart or let it fly right on by, depending on what feels right in our guts.

The Algebra of Unsolicited Parenting Advice

Back when I was a bright-eyed youngster, I fancied becoming a marine biologist. But let me tell you, when my high school algebra teacher started mixing letters with numbers, I quickly realized that path wasn't for me. I mean, come on, the letter A should be for apple, not some stand-in for a number! Despite this setback, I've come up with my own kind of algebra—a formula for sifting through all that unsolicited parenting advice that comes our way.

Here's the formula I use: Filter = (Source + Motive) x Prayer

Let's apply this to the situation involving my friend in the elevator. We'll use our formula to check the advice's source and motive and then run it through prayer to see what shakes out.

In this case, the source was a complete stranger, only aware of my friend's prominent baby bump. The motive seemed self-centered, as the stranger persisted with her incorrect assumption, even after my friend shared that her medical professionals had confirmed just one baby on board—four times over! Sometimes, yes, medical tests miss things, but with four confirming ultrasounds, we're talking about pretty solid evidence here.

Now, reflecting on how my friend responded—admittedly, it was more heated than necessary. That's often what happens when we're caught off guard. If she'd had a moment to process this interaction through prayer—even just a silent, "Lord, give me patience," or a lighthearted, "All right, Jesus, let's see how we handle this test"—she might have found a calmer, more collected response. Sometimes, the most powerful response is a moment of silence, allowing us a breath to gather our thoughts and proceed with grace.

This formula isn't just about handling advice; it's about managing our reactions in a way that aligns with who we aim to be—thoughtful, considerate, and anchored in faith. By filtering through source, motive, and prayer, we can navigate even the most unexpected or unwelcome advice without losing our cool.

All wisdom springs from God, yet sometimes, it can get twisted and misused down here on earth. How come? Well, we're living in a world that often pats you on the back for whatever feels good at the moment or justifies our knee-jerk reactions. But let's turn to what the Good Book says. James 3:17 tells us, "But the wisdom from above is first pure, then peaceable, gentle, open to reason, full of mercy and good fruits, impartial and sincere."

Y'all, I'll be the first to admit that I don't always have God front and center in every decision. Sometimes, I let the world's shiny offerings or the heat of the moment sway me more than I'd care to admit.

Now, I'm not telling you anything new when I say life's not a cakewalk. And for us tired mommas, it's even harder to catch our breath and truly grasp the weight of what's being thrown at us. There are times when you're just trying to wrap your head around a mess. You need a minute to pause, pray, and seek God's wisdom—knowing that's where true peace is found. Yet, there you are, fighting the urge to, let's say, "educate" someone with a bit more than your words. It's like walking a tightrope with no net below!

Over my last twenty-five years as a mom, I've had to check my desires against God's will more times than I can count. And let me tell you, the blessing of prayer and the healthy fear of a little thing called consequences have been my saving graces!

When you bow your head to pray for wisdom, keep in mind that true wisdom from God reflects His character. So, if you're trying to figure out if the guidance you've received is truly from above, just look for the divine fingerprints all over it. Sure, in algebra, A might sometimes equal three, but heavenly wisdom will always mirror the heart and nature of God.

Remember, Jesus knows and loves you and your family more deeply than you could ever imagine. Running the advice you receive through the filter of prayer is how you discern whether it's grounded in God's wisdom. Prayer not only helps in sorting good advice from bad, but it also shines a light on people's true intentions by revealing the heart behind their words.

All too often, we lose bits of our own spirit when we let worldly views cloud our vision. As parents, we're always learning and growing, but that doesn't mean we should let anyone dim our light or silence the unique voice God gave us.

I don't know what today looks like for you, but if you feel like you've lost pieces of yourself along the way, know that you aren't walking this path alone. There's a wellspring of hope because God is forever present, and He's in control. No matter where you find yourself in your journey—whether you've slipped up, strayed, or, like me, quit and restarted—He's right there, eager to connect with your heart and pour blessings into your life and your family's.

One of the things I cherish about the Lord is that He meets us exactly where we are. Sometimes, it might be a while between our chats with Him, and other times, it feels like I can't draw a breath without seeking His guidance.

Stay true to yourself, knowing God crafted you specifically to give your children everything they need. Your thoughts are important, and your feelings are valid—even when they might not be spot on. Guard your peace like it's a treasure.

We're all built for connection, but it's okay to stand firm when it comes to advocating for change, seeking resolutions, or pursuing peace, joy, and love for your family. Reflect on your feelings and emotions; if something doesn't sit right, take a moment to consider whether it's time for a change. If certain advice or influences bring unrest, it might be necessary to distance yourself from them, whether they're people or situations.

Sure, we can adapt and make concessions for the sake of harmony, but when you feel your core values beginning to drift, take a moment to stop and think about what you really want.

Ask yourself why. Evaluate whether your family's way of life is truly serving everyone's best interests. When you're clear on your stance, set solid boundaries around your core values and brace yourself—there might be some pushback. But hold fast because knowing and protecting your truth is worth every bit of the effort.

The more you lean into parenting according to your own expectations, the more you'll grow in confidence with your own style. Be gentle with yourself as you navigate this journey, and hang in there. Remember, anything truly worthwhile takes effort and grit.

I've learned that unsolicited parenting advice can be as pesky as an ornery old hen—it'll peck at you incessantly if you don't stand your ground.

But that's *only if you allow it*. Remember, you've got a choice in the matter.

Who wouldn't want to be a parent in today's world? The joys and blessings are boundless, so don't get caught up in living up to someone else's standards! Parent the children you have, not the ones you think you should have or the ones society might expect.

Ladies, it's up to you to decide what burdens you choose to bear. I encourage you to shed any advice that brings you anxiety or frustration or makes you feel judged, unworthy, or like a failure. Let it go! Drop it like the stinky diaper it is!

REFLECTIONS

Filtering with Faith: The Gideon Approach for Moms
Scripture Reading: Judges 6:36-40

Dear Momma, just like Gideon in the book of Judges, we too often need reassurance and guidance amidst our responsibilities. Gideon's method of seeking God's confirmation through the dew and the fleece (Judges 6:36-40) serves as a poignant metaphor for how we can approach the overwhelming advice we often encounter.

"Then Gideon said to God, 'If you will save Israel by my hand, as you have said, behold, I am laying a fleece of wool on the threshing floor. If there is dew on the fleece alone, and it is dry on all the ground, then I shall know that you will save Israel by my hand, as you have said.' And it was so" (Judges 6:36-38).

In the quiet hours of the evening, when the children are asleep and the house finally stills, you might find yourself reflecting on the multitude of advice you've received throughout the day. It's in these moments, much like Gideon with his fleece, that you can lay out your own "fleece" before the Lord—seeking His wisdom to filter through the voices and opinions that have piled up at your door.

The Need for a "Sheep Cloth Filter"

Just as Gideon used a simple piece of cloth to seek confirmation from God, you can use your "sheep cloth filter"—your prayer and discernment—to test the advice you receive. This filter isn't just for filtering out; it's for discerning what is truly beneficial and divinely appointed for your unique journey in motherhood.

Ask for Clarity: When Gideon asked for dew only on the fleece, he sought clarity from God. When advice comes your way, ask God to make it clear which pieces align with His will for you and your family. Pray for peace that surpasses understanding to guard your decisions (Philippians 4:6-7).

Seek Confirmation: Gideon needed confirmation not once but twice. It's okay to ask God for confirmation when you're making decisions based on the advice you've received. Seek signs in your daily life or through Scripture that affirm or warn against the paths laid out before you.

Embrace God's Guidance: Each step of Gideon's story reminds us that God is intimately involved in our journeys. Embrace the truth that God has a plan for you as a mom, and trust that He will equip you for every good work, just as He promised (2 Timothy 3:16-17).

Filter with Faith: Ultimately, Gideon's faith led him to victory. Let your faith guide you through the noisy world of parenting advice. Hold fast to what is good (1 Thessalonians 5:21), discarding what doesn't serve you or your family's spiritual and emotional growth.

As you navigate motherhood, remember that your "sheep cloth filter" is both a shield and a sieve—protecting you from unnecessary burdens while concentrating on the wisdom that truly matters. Like Gideon, may you find courage in the Lord's presence, assurance in His promises, and peace in His guidance.

Prayer

Lord, grant me the wisdom of Gideon to discern the advice I receive. Help me to lay out my fleece in prayer, seeking Your truth and confirmation. Equip me to filter through the voices, holding on to what is of You and letting go of what is not. May my journey in motherhood be a testament to Your faithfulness and guidance.

In Jesus' name,

Amen.

Small Group Discussion Questions

1. Why do some people feel the need to offer unsolicited parenting advice to others?

2. How can parents politely decline unsolicited advice without causing offense?
3. What are some common types of unsolicited parenting advice that parents receive?
4. Can unsolicited parenting advice ever be helpful, or is it always intrusive?
5. How can parents distinguish between well-meaning advice and judgmental criticism from others?

Self-Affirmations

- I approach family, friends, and strangers offering parenting advice with patience and understanding, recognizing that their intentions are often rooted in a desire to help.
- I confidently set boundaries and communicate my needs when it comes to receiving parenting advice, ensuring that my decisions as a parent are respected.
- I am secure in my role as a parent and trust my own judgment, knowing that I am best equipped to make decisions for my child's well-being.
- I choose to see unsolicited parenting advice as an opportunity for growth and learning, sifting through different perspectives to find what resonates with my values and parenting style.
- I am grateful for the support and love I receive from my family, friends, and even strangers, but I remain steadfast in my ability to make informed choices that prioritize my child's needs.

CHAPTER THREE
EXTERNAL INFLUENCES

Ever wondered if the world kinda sets moms up against each other because it profits from our struggles? After years of watching the same old patterns play out—from social media hype to societal pressures—I've noticed a troubling trend.

In this era of digital dazzle, we're spoon-fed images of perfection—snapshots of motherhood that are polished till they gleam. As we scroll through social media, it's all too easy to get caught up in trying to mimic these flawless moments, aiming to give our families what seems to be the best life. Yet, this pursuit often leaves us feeling detached from our own gritty, beautiful realities and the folks who make them worth living.

When we fall short of recreating these moments of supposed perfection, we often see ourselves and our loved ones as failures. This is the snare of modern motherhood narratives—it keeps us striving and never arriving, making sure those who set these impossible standards stay on top.

Every once in a while, a mom seems to break through the ordinary and snag the spotlight with her picture-perfect life and kids who never step out of line. We watch her, we envy her, and in her moments of glory, she becomes the model every mom aspires to be. But even she, hoisted high by the fickle winds of public approval, will eventually feel the sting of reality when the likes and comments stop providing the validation she craves.

Why chase a standard set by folks who don't even know us, pushing us toward an acceptance that's always just out of reach? Why give up our family's authenticity for a fleeting sense of belonging in a world that values conformity over genuine connection?

What if, instead, we toss aside society's yardstick and measure our lives by our own standards?

In this chapter, we're gonna dive deep into the world of parenting advice as seen through the lenses of social media and societal expectations. We'll unpack how these influences shape our parenting—from our inner peace to our children's futures—and how we can reclaim our identity as moms, setting a course that resonates with our true selves.

Unsolicited Parenting Advice on Social Media

Do y'all remember those popular kids back in high school? They were the ones who were as pretty as a peach and smooth as a Sunday sermon, making the rest of us green with envy. Everyone either wanted to be them or be with them, thinking maybe some of that golden glow might just rub off on us. We all thought if we could just walk a mile in their shoes, life would be as sweet as pie. Behind those shiny smiles, though, some of them were battling demons we couldn't see, wrestling with troubles deeper than the river.

And there we were, counting the days till graduation, thinking we'd leave all that high school hoopla behind for a grown-up world brimming with real substance and true grit.

Well, were we ever wrong! Turns out, that same old high school hierarchy didn't disappear; it followed us through college, career, and right into the thick of parenting. Ever find yourself feeling that sting of disappointment when you realized the adult social ladder wasn't just alive but kicking harder than a mule, especially on social media where climbing up seems to cost more than ever?

Historically, every society has had its own pecking order—a way to see who's who based on what they wore or how they carried themselves. Before the days of the internet, places like the town square or city gates were where folks gathered to catch up, swap stories, and share advice—kind of like the ancient version of a Facebook feed.

Back in biblical times, the city gate wasn't just a place to pass through—it was the spot to be if you wanted to be in the know. It's where the lady from Proverbs 31 shined like a new penny. She was everything a woman could aspire to be—beautiful, savvy, and kind-hearted. Her husband was considered blessed just for being hitched to her.

But here's a little morsel for thought about that Proverbs 31 gal that might stick in your craw: She wasn't real.

Proverbs 31 was penned by the mother of a king, outlining the virtues to seek in a noble wife. It's likely that Bathsheba, King Solomon's mom, embodied these very traits, inspiring this chapter as a timeless guide for all of God's daughters. While she sets the bar high as the epitome of an ideal woman, remember, she's not a real, flesh-and-blood figure walking among us.

Now, y'all, achieving the Proverbs 31 standard isn't a walk in the park. There might be moments you feel like you're just about there, climbing that mountain of virtues, and then—bless your heart—you might just slip a bit. She's there for us to look up to, to stretch toward, not to beat ourselves up over when we stumble and miss the mark.

Even though these virtues have stood the test of time, in today's world, with the never-ending, rapid-fire pace of social media, our ideas of womanhood are more jumbled up than a cat in a yarn basket.

Added to that mix is the constant barrage of selfies. As each new momma flips through her social media feeds, she's bombarded with images of other moms in seemingly perfect snapshots. We all ache for that kind of picture-perfect validation, dreaming of capturing our own glossy, magazine-worthy moments of motherhood. We yearn for scenes that show the world the kind of mom we strive to be, with a pristine, picturesque setting and those darling, spotless kiddos looking up at us in adoration.

Oh, how we yearn to capture those serene moments holding our babies as they nod off to sleep, to record their first wobbly steps, and to catch that sweet "I love you, Mommy," spoken clear as a bell into the mic for us to cherish forever.

And isn't it just like every mom to dream up the perfect family vacation, timed just right to snap photos for the annual Christmas card? We might not say it out loud, but those pictures sure do scream, "Look at us! We made it happen!"

These golden slices of motherhood make every hard day worth it, but boy, do we sometimes overlook the circus that goes into setting up those picture-perfect moments. Take this one time, for instance, when I got it in my head to have a beachside photo shoot during a family trip to Florida. I was all set to get those ideal Christmas card pictures of my downright adorable family. But let me tell you, I wasn't ready for the comedy of errors that unfolded.

I'd booked us a pretty little beach house and lapped up every bit of advice I could for making that twenty-hour drive a hoot and a half. I spent two whole weeks planning—packing snacks like a pro, plotting out every bathroom stop, and loading up on enough games and movies to run a small theater.

But despite my best-laid plans, the kids were still kids—looking at each other enough to cause squabbles and touching each other just enough to declare sibling war. Regrettably, blinders are only for horses, and my husband vetoed my joke about leaving the kids at a rest stop for Grandma and Grandpa to pick up. All I could do was try to soothe their squawks of "She's looking at me!" and "He's touching me!"

And wouldn't you know it? The one thing I forgot was a giant bottle of ibuprofen because that headache of mine decided to set up camp as soon as we hit the road. By the time we rolled into that beach house driveway, any notions of exemplary behavior had been dropped off back at the Georgia state line. Writing this now, I can't help but laugh (and cringe) at the memories!

The next morning was set for our big photo shoot, but I quickly realized I'd underestimated just how worn out that long drive would have us all. We managed a quick breakfast, ran a few errands, and then the kids took a short nap while I ironed everyone's matching white outfits. Once they woke, I fixed their hair, popped them into their outfits, touched up my makeup, and off we went to catch that perfect sunset glow on the beach.

Our photographer was on a tight schedule with another family right after us, so I was all fired up to snag those Christmas card-worthy shots pronto. She set us up just right, backs against the sand dunes, the wind tickling our faces just so. There we were, my beautiful family, arrayed on the sand in crisp whites, with the boys in checkered shirts that matched the blanket under us. And that gentle breeze in our hair? Picture perfect.

Well, that lasted all of twenty minutes before the tide turned, and my sleepy, hungry kiddos started to check out. I had snacks and juice boxes at the ready—because what momma doesn't? But I hadn't planned for the travel weariness, a curious lizard, and, yep, bird poop right outta nowhere. Who could have?

The kids had about had it with sitting still and smiling. My plans crumbled along with my daughter's composure when a gust flipped the blanket's edge, sprinkling sand all over her little toes.

That's when Austin spotted a lizard lounging on a nearby log, and y'all, that was the end of any semblance of order. The chase was on, ending with a log flipping and my boy face-planting into the sand.

But I was bound and determined, come heck or high water, to get that picture-perfect moment. After scooping up Austin and dusting him off, we regrouped for a full family shot just as the wind decided to show off again. What started as a gentle caress quickly turned into a wild whirl, flinging my hair every which way till it nearly blinded me. While I wrestled my hair into submission with a clip, the older boys gave up and dove back into their video games.

Then came the downpour—nope, not a single heavenly sprinkle in sight!

The sky was clear, but there we were, in the midst of a full-on bombardment as the wind ushered in a bold flock of seagulls. Yep, you heard right, girls—the seagulls unleashed their own little storm right during our photo shoot.

But I'm calling it a win anyway! In one miraculous snap, we captured a scene that looked straight out of a social media highlight reel, and out of the chaos, a Christmas card star was born. And let me tell you, I earned some serious brownie points with the Good Lord because no seagulls or lizards suffered in the making of our holiday masterpiece! Though, I can't promise I haven't considered revenge on their descendants over the years.

Fitting the Mold

Friends, please tell me I'm not the only one who dreams of a peaceful vacation with grateful, well-mannered kiddos—is that too much to ask? Reflecting on that beachside photo fiasco, I wash my hands of any responsibility for the day's calamity.

Nope, I lay that blame right at the feet of social media's golden gates, luring us over the bridge of no return and into the hands of their almighty algorithm!

Y'all, I bought into the hype, hook, line, and sinker. I was duped by the allure of adoration through hearts, likes, and gushing comments! It's that darn tempting force that overtakes our senses, messing with how we think and act. And let me tell you, it was every dopamine-fueled hit from those likes and shares that drove me right to the edge of lizard-chasing, bird-dodging madness!

If it weren't for social media planting the seed, the notion that a single photo could define my worth as a momma would've never crossed my mind. But there I was, scrolling and comparing, caught up in the fantasy of living up to every picture-perfect, social media-crafted Christmas card snapshot.

Just like my hair in that wild Florida wind, I found myself swayed by those picture-perfect family images splashed across social media. They captured fun, inventive poses and magical moments that screamed pure joy. My heart sank a bit with each scroll; I felt like I was failing, not just as a momma but as the family's unofficial historian.

How had I missed the memo that every baby's first birthday photo needs a floating bouquet of whimsical flowers? And what kind of hostess was I, letting guests leave without monogrammed party favors? After all, who even hands out Pez dispensers, glow-in-the-dark bracelets, or simple sticker sheets anymore? Clearly, my parenting playbook needed a major overhaul.

That was it—no more feeling like my parenting was a few steps behind. It was high time to step up my game. So, I decided to redefine what it meant to capture our family's journey. Christmas photos in front of a tree? That was so last century. No, sir, my family was going to grace the cover of every motherhood magazine, styled like winged angels perched atop a Christmas tree!

I traded my genuine motherhood moments for a subscription to society's glossy, picture-perfect family ideal. Instead of being truly present with my kids, I found myself staging each moment for social media glory. And in that chase for perfection, I placed a higher value on pretense than on those spontaneous, loving memories that truly mattered.

Looking back on that beach photo shoot, it's all too clear. Friends and family glanced at our Christmas card, murmured a polite "Oh, how lovely," and pinned it up with the others until January. Then, it likely found its way into the trash or got buried in a box under the stairs, lost in the shadows until next year's cleaning spree.

Yes, we captured that frame-able moment, but what truly resonates with me now is the memory of the whole shebang. We found joy in the chaos, from playing with the local wildlife to learning everyone's quick duck-and-cover move at the first squawk of a seagull. And even though it didn't make it to film, we all remember what Austin looked like with a face full of sand! I've come to realize that the most meaningful pictures are the ones that don't make it to social media. They're captured in those fleeting moments of vulnerability, echoed in the screams or laughter carried on the wind, and in those intense emotional bursts that come from unexpected surprises that draw us closer as a family.

Now, more than ever, moms are bombarded with a torrent of information, so much so that it can be downright overwhelming to sift the meaningful from the mundane. And don't get me wrong, there's absolutely nothing amiss with capturing staged moments of sheer adorableness, feats of prowess, or dreamy family vacations! I still wrangle up the kiddos for what I call "Forced Family Fun Photos." But nowadays, it's on our terms, for our joy. That's where the difference lies. The idea wasn't the problem—it was the intent behind it. I needed to value our intentions and experiences more than the opinions flung at us by social media.

We must stand firm in knowing who we are so we aren't easily swayed from our family's course. If we're focused on content that stays true to ourselves, it's tougher to be thrown off track or suckered into society's pressurized mold of what a family ought to look like.

So, I urge you to take a moment to reflect on your values, expectations, and the vision you have for your family before you let social media have a say. Don't let it mute who you are or who you aspire to be as a momma.

A Birthday Bash to Remember

Even though social media sparked the beach photo shoot idea, we get bombarded with advice from all corners, both voiced and silent, direct and implied. It's just the way of the world, every culture's method for doling out what's expected. We're soaking up how-to-live tips from the get-go, most of the time not even realizing it until something comes along and knocks the wind out of our sails.

Often, it's not even advice per se, but we might take it that way. Like getting tugged at the heartstrings by a sentimental ad or someone's tear-jerking tale. Or maybe it's less subtle, like the sting of a sharp comment or the unspoken judgment in a deep sigh or a rolling eye.

I had one of those moments at my little Brooklynn's first birthday bash. She's my only girl, and I was all set to make her feel like the belle of the ball. I went all out on a fancy dress, imagining her little grin and that sparkle in her eye as she saw herself all dolled up in the mirror. She pranced about, clearly thrilled, twirling in her dress as our nearest and dearest cooed and clicked away with their cameras.

Then, the whispers started. I caught a few sideways glances and overheard: "You know she'll never wear that dress again, and she won't even remember this." There was Brooklynn, cake-smudged face and all, while someone chuckled, "Oh, my! Andrea, honey, that's why my kids wear old clothes to their parties!" But the zinger that really got to me was a loudly whispered, "I don't know why she bothered with that fancy dress. She's just gonna cover it with a bib. You won't even see it in the pictures!" As if to say my choice was frivolous or that I lacked the sense to make a wise decision for my child.

One second, I was basking in the joy of watching my baby girl shine like royalty, and the next, I was feeling deflated, second-guessing my decision, all because of a few thoughtless remarks.

It seems like there's always someone ready to rain on your parade, even as they're reaching for your candy. That fancy dress was chosen as a sparkling highlight for a milestone in our family's journey. Yet, in the midst of it all, I let the unsolicited and even unspoken advice from a naysayer chip away at my joy.

For a good while, my memories of that day were shadowed with a bit of sadness because someone had to go and drop their unwanted opinions right into the middle of my daughter's special day. All I aimed for was to wrap my little girl in love, make her day unforgettable, and snap those precious photos surrounded by family who cherished her. And when I think back, it's those moments of her twinkling eyes, watching us all doting on her, that I hold dear.

But here's a little twist to the tale: That dress is safely tucked away, awaiting the day it can be worn by my first granddaughter. And that's exactly why I planned for a bib! That critic didn't know the full story or see the long-term vision I had for my family. What they dismissed as frivolous was actually steeped in thought and care.

Reflecting now, I realize I could have shrugged off those comments better in the moment. Sure, I couldn't stop the sideways looks or the whispers, but I didn't have to let them dim my joy.

Steven Covey's tale about the father with unruly kids on the subway sure strikes a chord about being patient with youngsters, but let's paint the full picture. What if that weary passenger who snapped had just come off a double shift and was nursing a raging migraine?

We've all caught those glances from fellow shoppers when our little one pitches a fit over candy bars at the checkout. But those looks? They might not be judgments. That cranky lady shooting you the stink eye?

She might be fighting her own battles. And just because your little darlin' danced on her last frayed nerve doesn't mean she's passing judgment on your parenting. Mommas, we ought to dish out the same kind of understanding we're wishing for, trying our best to lead with grace, even when we feel the weight of those stares. Trust me, I've been there more times than I can count, and I'm still not holding a trophy for patience!

If you're doing your best with your kids on a tough day, let that onlooker's frown slide right off you. It's likely their own struggle is sparking that glare, not something you've done, so don't let it sour your day.

Three Unconscious Biases Shaped by Unsolicited Advice

Sometimes, the advice we think we hear isn't even about what we're doing; it's about unconscious biases sneaking into the mix.

Biases act like invisible signposts guiding our decisions, often without us even realizing it. These mental shortcuts help us navigate the complexities of life, but they can sometimes lead us astray, especially when they're formed through the subtle, unsolicited advice that seeps into our parenting.

From the moment our children enter this world, they start absorbing the subtle cues and norms that swirl around them—many of which come packed with implicit biases. This unsolicited guidance isn't always spoken aloud; it often comes through in the expectations and assumptions others make about how we should raise our kids.

In this section, we'll dig into how these unconscious biases, rooted in the often well-meaning but unasked-for advice from those around us, can shape our children's self-esteem and even influence their future career paths. Recognizing these biases helps us actively choose which influences we allow to shape our parenting and which ones we let slide right off our backs like water off a duck. Our aim is to foster a home where our children can thrive, uninhibited by the limiting beliefs society might try to impose on them.

Gender Bias

Lauren's daughter, Reagan, was quite the tomboy, much to the joy of her parents. Unlike the little girls twirling in tutus, Reagan was more at home in the mud, playing flag football with the neighborhood boys, practicing karate, or joining her dad on hunting trips. From kindergarten through high school, Reagan embraced these passions, learning valuable lessons in teamwork, leadership, and resilience along the way.

However, not everyone was on board with Reagan's less traditional interests. Lauren still recalls the sting from a conversation with her own mother when she invited her to one of Reagan's third-grade football games. Her mother hesitated, then awkwardly replied, "I have to work that day. Why can't she do something more . . . I mean . . . Well, something more . . . feminine?"

Despite Reagan's enthusiasm and the inclusive nature of her team, this lack of support from a family member brought unwelcome doubts and hurt. After that conversation, Lauren decided not to invite her mother to any more of Reagan's games or share her achievements in hunting and karate.

This situation highlights a clear case of gender bias, where Grandma's expectations for more "feminine" activities were at odds with Reagan's true interests. Lauren chose to support her daughter's passions rather than conform to outdated stereotypes, which unfortunately resulted in a gap between Reagan and her grandmother. This chasm, widened by unspoken expectations and unsolicited advice, became a lasting rift, depriving Grandma of the chance to truly appreciate her strong, talented, and independent granddaughter.

Beauty Bias

Beauty bias is this sneaky stereotype dictating what beauty should look like, suggesting that folks who fit this mold are somehow better than the rest. It's a classic case of comparison bias, where we judge our own worth by stacking it up against others.

Nowadays, graphic editors, with a little help from artificial intelligence, can spin reality into pure fantasy. I kid you not, I once stumbled across a video on social media where a piece of pepperoni pizza was transformed into a swimsuit supermodel. Yes, you heard that right—a pizza! It's wild what you can find floating around the internet these days, from YouTube to Facebook, showcasing these digital makeovers.

Imagine handing a graphic designer something as mundane as your trash and watching them turn it into what many would call a treasure. But let's be clear—just because something looks like a treasure doesn't mean it holds true value, especially when it's built on a foundation of deception. The old saying, "One man's trash is another man's treasure," really misses the mark here, as these transformations set unrealistic standards for beauty and worth.

Every snapshot you scroll past on social media, every seemingly perfect family portrait, comes with its own set of filters. They make life seem a bit shinier and more beautiful than it might be in the harsh light of day. Even those moments that seem candid and raw are often retouched to perfection.

This culture of fake, airbrushed images serves up implicit advice through beauty bias and comparison. Growing up, I remember how magazine images shaped my own perceptions of beauty and worth, making me feel like I never quite measured up. Determined to shield my kids from these demoralizing effects as much as possible, I've made it a point to challenge these unrealistic standards, encouraging them to value the beauty of real, unfiltered life.

I aimed to raise my sons and daughter to value individuals for their character, the kindness in their hearts, and how they engage with the world, not just the superficial standards often plastered across glossy magazine pages or flashy advertisements. To curb the influence of idealized beauty and overt sexualization, I made the decision to keep our home free of mainstream magazines, allowing only kid-friendly educational publications. We approached all forms of media—including social media and television programs that discuss health, body image, or fashion—with a critical eye, being particularly mindful of how they portray individuals, especially women. But if you recall my Christmas card story, I, too, fell victim to the lure and immeasurable standard of these images.

Beauty bias is rampant, and inevitably, our kids will feel where they supposedly fall short by comparison. It's our parental duty to illuminate the manipulative tactics behind media images, trends, and societal expectations and to guide them in understanding the true essence and value of beauty—this is as crucial for boys as it is for girls. Whenever we encounter seemingly perfect images, we ought to question the standards set: Is this realistic, or is it digitally concocted? What are the values we hold dear? Are we inadvertently trading our self-worth for a contrived image, akin to valuing ourselves as mere pieces of pizza?

If we unwittingly chase after this fantasy of a perfect family, our children will also feel compelled to live up to this impossible standard, which breeds a persistent sense of inadequacy. It's crucial to recognize these moments. Are you unintentionally instilling a sense of insufficiency in your children by valuing deceptive portrayals of life?

Are you and your family slowly morphing into mere projections, akin to a pizza dressed up as a model? This transformation can creep up gradually or happen overnight, so staying vigilant and conscious of these influences is essential.

Don't just swallow everything you see hook, line, and sinker. Take a moment to really look at what's unfolding before you. Reflect on what truly matters to you and your brood so you can kindly toss aside anything that doesn't square with your family's values.

Career Bias

Career bias can start nudging on our choices early, often setting in before our little ones even hit preschool. It's the kind of belief that success and true happiness can only come from certain careers—those well-paved paths like law, medicine, or engineering.

Think about it—what pops into your mind when you hear "starving artist"? Probably a vision of a youthful soul, brush in hand, lost in their canvas during their college days, only to wind up struggling to make ends meet. It's a tough image to shake.

How many of y'all have tucked away dreams of a creative career because it seemed too far out there, too risky? As someone who's spent years on the edge of songwriting, singing, and writing myself, I've danced with this fear a time or two.

This stereotype—this career bias—has a grip on a lot of good folks. It holds back parents from encouraging their kids to chase dreams of becoming musicians, painters, or writers. Driven by the fear of their kids facing a life of scraping by, many parents nudge their kids toward careers they see as safer bets.

And here's the twist—the very parents who push practicality often end up as the misunderstood antagonists in the memoirs of some of the most successful folks in the arts. Those artists who do make it big? We look up to them, imagining their lives filled with glam and glitter, not the struggles they faced getting there.

The notion of a "starving artist" paints a grim picture of failure for those pursuing creative careers, suggesting a destiny of hardship and struggle just for following their passion. Yet, success is not a one-size-fits-all scenario. Believe it or not, there are creatives out there who might not be lighting up billboards but are living contentedly, perhaps more fulfilled than if they were chasing big bucks in high-stakes finance.

We've touched on three unconscious biases, but the truth is, the world's got a whole mess more. Each bias that unfolds is influenced by the values and resources of our communities and families.

These sneaky biases, whether we realize it or not, can twist our preferences, judgments, and decisions. Instead of taking these biases at face value, we must pray and reflect deeply on what truly serves our loved ones best.

For instance, when we blindly follow advice that doesn't echo our values, we risk shifting the very foundations of our family's beliefs. Take home ownership—it's often pitched as a symbol of independence and stability. Yet, success and stability don't look the same for everyone.

Plenty of perfectly stable and successful folks find freedom in renting, choosing flexibility over the hefty responsibilities of property upkeep.

Each decision, like whether to rent or buy, crafts the unique tapestry of your family's experience. With every nugget of advice that comes your way, weigh it against your family's values. Ask yourself: Does this advice pave a path that aligns with what truly matters to us?

Shaped by Personal Experiences

When both a banana and an apple tumble from the countertop, they end up bruised, but differently so, due to the uniqueness of their skins and fruit within. It dawned on me that we, too, can endure the same challenges yet bear our bruises distinctively.

In a similar way, our past—both its highs and its scars—travels with us. The emotional tapestry of our childbirth experiences, in particular, can profoundly shape our parenting. Delivering a baby is challenging enough without adding the strain of a traumatic experience into the mix.

Our life's encounters tint our perceptions and reactions. Certain moments test us deeply, threatening to break us if we let them. Since our external experiences and inner perceptions are unique, our bruises won't mirror anyone else's, nor should they.

Each woman processes life's events in her own way. The emotional and mental weights we carry as we raise our children are substantial and often undervalued. These experiences—these memories and emotions—are significant. They evolve over time and play a crucial role in shaping who we are and how we parent.

The journey of learning is deeply personal, filled with moments and challenges unique to each of us. My own journey was marked with a pretty big bruise by the birth of my son, Cameron. His delivery left a profound imprint on me, especially since he was rushed to the NICU immediately after revival. Processing the trauma took years, and the challenges continued as he was later diagnosed with cerebral palsy.

My dream of peaceful, idyllic moments gazing into my newborn's eyes was shattered. The reality was far from the cozy, picture-perfect scenes I had envisioned. Even after enduring two miscarriages and welcoming two sons, the shock of the past lingered heavily when I discovered I was pregnant with a daughter.

Fueled by the pervasive advice about mother-daughter bonds, I envisioned a little girl who would adore me—a best friend for life. I dreamed of beach trips, holding hands as we collected seashells and sharing laughs over manicures and ice cream. But reality taught me to temper my expectations, as each child's story—and our bruises—are uniquely our own.

Instead, I found myself the momma of a daddy's girl who seemed to have no need for me in her early years. All around me, well-meaning folks dished out advice on how to forge a bond with my daughter, but nothing seemed to take hold. Honestly, I not only blamed myself, but I also felt I deserved it, considering the bonding struggles I faced with Cameron. The thought that maybe no little girl would want a momma like me haunted my heart.

When we fall short of our own expectations or those set by others, it's all too easy to label ourselves failures and carry that burden around. But here's the thing—your experiences craft your belief system, shaping how you respond and advance in life. You can't expect me to parent as if I haven't faced trauma, just as I can't expect you to parent without the influences of your past.

God crafted each of us to parent according to the journey we've walked. My trials and triumphs have shaped me into the mom I am—imperfect but precisely what my children need. I can't be you. I can't raise your kids because I don't possess what they require. That's your role, tailored by God for you alone.

There Are No Binkies in the Bible

I once stumbled across a social media saga about a momma trying to wean her toddler off his binky. Would you believe there were nearly three hundred comments under that post? Just about binkies! Some folks were downright ornery, but a few shared some legitimately funny strategies.

One momma got creative—she told her kiddo they were planting his binkies in a pot in the backyard. While the little tyke napped, she swapped the pot for one with flowers blooming. That boy woke up to find his binkies had "grown" into a bouquet! Another savvy mom gave her child's binkie a send-off fit for a king, complete with a tiny stuffed elephant standing guard over the makeshift grave.

Oh, the stories made me chuckle, reminding me of the lengths I went to with my four kids. All those fibs—yes, they're all fun fibs—but when you're a momma hanging by a thread, sometimes you have to get creative to snag a moment of peace.

To those tykes, a binky is more than just a piece of plastic; it's a little piece of heaven. It stands for safety, security, and comfort. And here we are, turning their trusty binkies into tall tales of blooming flowers and graveyards. It might baffle the little ones—flowers growing from binkies, really? But hey, if it works, it works, and that momma sure did get creative!

I'm not judging because I'm also not innocent. Take the time my daughter caught me red-handed, playing the tooth fairy. Caught off guard, I told her that the tooth fairy delegated moms to inspect the teeth to ensure they had been taken care of. I assured her she'd done a fine job and the tooth fairy would surely drop by with some coins once she was asleep. I'm still waiting on that quality assurance paycheck from the tooth fairy, mind you. Now, every time my daughter gets a cavity, I half wonder if it's the tooth fairy's way of getting back at me for getting creative!

I know we want to weave wonderful tales for our children. Our momma's heart aims to shield their innocence and nurture their sense of wonder, but only up to the point it doesn't turn them into a target for teasing. But where in the Good Book does it say a child must be weaned off the binky by age three? I've scoured the Bible—even the Message version—and not a whisper of "binky" is to be found.

So why all the fuss? Who decreed that by such and such an age, certain things must happen? It's society or sometimes doctors if there's a medical reason, but mostly, it's those sideways glances and whispered judgments at playgroups that pressure us.

And there we go again, parenting according to someone else's script, swayed by others' opinions, weaving tales and pulling strings, convinced that these strangers know what's best for our kids better than we do.

As moms, we fret that if our kids don't hit certain milestones by the "accepted" time, they'll forever be playing catch-up, never quite fitting into the molds set by society and the polished veneers of social media.

Milestones are merely suggestions, not gospel truth. There's no proven link between mastering the potty at eighteen months and soaring to the top later in life. I've never stumbled across a college application curious about when you ditched your binky. Truth is, whether your kiddo was the last in the playgroup to say goodbye to their pacifier or the first, they're just as capable of blossoming into their fullest potential.

Folks, we need to seek guidance from above, listen to our hearts, and trust that momma intuition when it whispers, "Something's off here." While we might try to script every step of our children's lives, the honest truth is we don't hold the reins as tightly as we think. Our role isn't to choreograph every developmental stage; it's to support and nudge our little ones toward fresh adventures.

As I learn to let go of my need to control everything in my life and my kids' lives, the Lord gently reminds me, "Hey there, settle down. You're not the one writing this narrative. It's My story. I'm crafting it for you, fulfilling the purpose I've planted within you." I need that nudge from God daily, sometimes hourly—such is the journey of parenthood.

To all the mommas out there feeling weighed down by the binky brigade, hear me loud and clear: you're doing wonderfully. It's tough, but you're doing your best with what you've got. Nobody understands your child quite like you do, so lean into that gut feeling you've got.

Like many others, I've let harsh self-critique colored by others' standards cloud my judgment, making me feel less than. We shouldn't let external pressures shape how we see ourselves or our parenting. Trust in your unique journey with your kids because, momma, you know best.

Why do we often piece together our lives using snapshots of perfection, aligning them with cultural norms, when we know full well we've outgrown these one-size-fits-all expectations? It's like we're still carrying around an old blanket that doesn't cover us anymore.

It's crucial we tailor advice to fit our family's unique values and beliefs. Honey, if God intended you to be a banana, you can't force yourself into being an apple, no matter how hard you try. Embrace who you are because that role is yours alone, and don't try to be me because I'm already taken—I've got my own dance to do.

Mental Health on External Unsolicited Parenting Advice

Mental health can really take a hit from all that unsolicited parenting advice we get. It's like double trouble—what we see on social media and what society expects of us. If we're not careful, we let these external forces have too much say in how we see ourselves as moms, handing over the reins of how we think and act.

Carrying the weight of all that advice can really drag us down into a pit of criticism and self-doubt, leaving us struggling with feelings of judgment, perfectionism, jealousy, and guilt.

Have you ever picked up a shiny apple at the store only to find it's bruised on the other side? Well, people are kinda like that too. We might only see their shiny moments, completely missing the bruises they're hiding.

The thing is, when we're always comparing ourselves and finding faults, we drift away from what really matters—leaning on God and fulfilling the purpose He's got for us. Instead, we get hung up on every little flaw, real or imagined.

Social media doesn't help, making us feel like our lives are just not up to snuff compared to everyone else's highlight reels. We end up chasing after moments we didn't even know we wanted until we saw someone else living them.

And if we get too caught up in meeting everyone else's expectations or climbing to the top of our social feed, that drive for perfection can really skew our intentions into something downright unachievable. Yet, we keep on chasing, thinking perfection equals happiness.

Dreaming and hoping for better is part of life, and sometimes God uses others to give us a nudge. But when that yearning turns into obsession, we're stepping over a line, breaking the tenth commandment without even realizing it.

"You shall not covet your neighbor's house; you shall not covet your neighbor's wife, or his male servant, or his female servant, or his ox, or his donkey, or anything that is your neighbor's" (Exodus 20:17).

Coveting—now that's a word that packs a punch. It means having a mighty strong desire for something that someone else has—wanting it so badly that it might just cross the line into being wrong. God put this right up there on His list of no-nos—His top ten sins, if you will.

With jealousy comes a whole mess of guilt about our own shortcomings and, yep, guilt for feeling jealous too. Sure, a little remorse can help us learn from our mistakes, but guilt? It can drag us down into a dark and heavy place if we let it.

Y'all, according to some statistics, there've been hundreds of folks who've lost their lives and thousands who've been hurt doing things for social media—taking selfies, pulling stunts, you name it. The United States ranks high in these tragic numbers, with folks dying from things like suffocation, electrocution, falls, and more because they were chasing that perfect shot.

But can you recall the names of any of these people who died?

Sadly, me neither.

It's a stark reminder, isn't it? We get so caught up trying to capture a life that looks good from the outside that we risk missing what's truly valuable. At the end of the day, those social media platforms don't have a lick of care about what happens to you or yours. We're all just stories passing by, with folks scrolling until something else catches their eye.

So tell me, what are you willing to trade for a thumbs-up? Are you gonna let those precious ones you love suffer just for a heart emoji? Who really holds your heart, and whose hands matter the most to you?

Navigating motherhood is like riding a rollercoaster—some days, you're the queen of the castle, slaying it in that Super-Mom cape. The house sparkles, dinner's on the table by six, and you remember each one of your kids' names come bedtime.

But then there are those days when all you wanna do is stay in your pajamas, make sock puppets, and let the kiddos have dry cereal for supper. And that's just fine. Embrace it and shed that guilt.

Every momma is riding her own journey of learning and balancing. Why let someone who doesn't even know you slap a label of failure on your forehead? Why give outsiders a spot in your mind, weighing you down with their judgments?

Cut yourself some slack, darlin'. We ought to treat ourselves with the same kindness we'd show to anyone else. Allow yourself to stumble without getting all torn up over it. Just wake up each day aiming to do your best.

Take it one day at a time, sifting through the advice—toss out what doesn't fit and keep what shines. Step off that comparison merry-go-round so the mental toll doesn't start eating at you. Don't let social media skew your vision of the mom you're meant to be.

Remember, Jesus gave it all for us. He loves us through and through, no matter the mess.

If you catch yourself in the jaws of comparison, remember only Jesus reached perfection. Happiness isn't a place to get to; it's found in walking alongside Him through this life. Don't waste your days trying to live out someone else's snapshot.

Instead of pining over what you don't have, focus on what really counts for you and yours. Be proud of who you are, and raise those kiddos to go out and make their own way.

And shake off that mom guilt right now, will ya? Let your kids know they're your joy, your pride. Share not just the wins but also the stumbles—teach them that every bit of life is packed with lessons.

Love, laughter, and the memories you make—that's the true treasure. And those kiddos? They're the followers who matter most. So cherish every single moment you get to spend with them.

REFLECTIONS

The Real Beauty of the Proverbs 31 Woman
Scripture Reading: Proverbs 31:10-31

As we explore the emblematic Proverbs 31 woman, it's easy to feel like we're falling short of an unattainable ideal. This passage, often held as the gold standard for godly womanhood, can seem more like a lofty burden than an encouragement. But let's peel back the layers and discover the heart of the message tailored for you, a real mom in today's world.

Proverbs 31:10-31 describes a woman of noble character, one who is industrious, compassionate, and wise. Yet, it's crucial to remember that these verses were originally written as an acrostic poem meant to celebrate womanhood, not to serve as a checklist for perfection.

Verses 25-26 say, "Strength and dignity are her clothing, and she laughs at the time to come. She opens her mouth with wisdom, and the teaching of kindness is on her tongue." Here, the true essence of the Proverbs 31 woman shines through—it's not about her achievements or tasks but her character.

As modern-day mommas, the pressure of comparison can sneak into our hearts through every swipe on social media or well-meaning comment from others. Yet God doesn't call you to be a carbon copy of anyone else, not even the Proverbs 31 woman.

Consider **2 Corinthians 10:12**: "But when they measure themselves by one another and compare themselves with one another, they are without understanding." God reminds us that our worth isn't found in comparison but in our unique creation in His image.

Wisdom Over Tasks: She speaks with wisdom and kindness—attributes that outshine any perfectly executed task. In what ways can you incorporate more wisdom and kindness in your communications, both within your home and in the community?

Laughter and Joy: She laughs without fear of the future. How can you cultivate a spirit of joy and trust in God's plan for your life, even when the days are long and challenges arise?

Momma, remember, you are more than enough because of whose you are, not because of what you do. The Proverbs 31 woman isn't a rival in the race of life; she's a fellow traveler pointing us toward a life of purpose and peace in God.

Prayer

Lord, thank You for the beautiful example of the Proverbs 31 woman. Help me to see her as a source of inspiration, not intimidation. Remind me that my value in Your eyes comes not from what I accomplish but from who I am in You. Grant me the strength to embody wisdom and kindness and the grace to laugh at the days to come, trusting in Your perfect plan for me and my family.

In Jesus' name,

Amen.

Small Group Discussion Questions

1. How does the description of the Proverbs 31 woman make you feel about your own day-to-day activities? Do you find it inspiring or intimidating?

2. In what ways has the culture of comparison affected your view of yourself and your parenting? How can you combat the pressures of social media and societal expectations in your life?

3. Discuss a time when you felt pressured to meet an unrealistic standard. How did it affect your mental health and your relationship with your family?

4. What are some practical ways you can clothe yourself in strength and dignity in the midst of your busy life as a mom?

5. Share a situation where you found it challenging to respond with wisdom and kindness. What did you learn from that experience?

6. The Proverbs 31 woman "laughs at the time to come." How can you find joy and laughter in your role as a mom despite the uncertainties and challenges?

7. How can focusing on your spiritual growth impact your ability to live out the virtues of the Proverbs 31 woman in modern times?

8. Discuss how you can prioritize character and values over achievements and appearances in your family. What changes might you need to make to align more closely with these priorities?

Self-Care Affirmations

- I am doing my best, and that is enough.
- I am more than the sum of my daily tasks and responsibilities.
- I choose to celebrate my victories, no matter how small they seem.
- I release the need for perfection and embrace my real, imperfect journey.
- I trust my intuition and make parenting decisions that feel right for my family.
- I give myself permission to rest and recharge, knowing it makes me a better mom.

CHAPTER FOUR
EVALUATING THE ADVICE

Advice should make us better, but along my journey as a mom, I realized I was parenting according to what others thought was right until I became just a faint reflection of the mom I wanted to be. I made a firm vow that from that moment on, my time as a mom would truly reflect what I felt was best for me and my kids. Once I got the hang of filtering advice by its source and discerning the intention behind it, then through prayer, I began to discern how to weigh that advice—whether it was something to consider or just blaring noise to let go of as I walked away.

So far, you've learned to recognize what unsolicited advice is, where it comes from, and what it can do to you. Now that we've clearly defined the problem, let's get to work on what we can do about it.

Let's start with a moment that got on my very last nerve with one of my boys. There was this time when Austin wanted to go off with a buddy to do something I wasn't too crazy about and didn't agree with. He tried to convince me it was okay because other parents were on board. I came back at him with the classic mom line—"Just because everyone else is doing it doesn't make it right"—but by the end, my boy and his analytical mind actually showed me a thing or two about sifting through the noise of unsolicited advice.

So here's how that conversation went down:

> Austin: "Why not, Mom? Other kids are going, so it's gotta be okay. It's fine!"
>
> Me: "Austin, if all your friends decided to jump off a bridge, would you do it too?"
>
> Austin: "Depends. Who's on the bridge with me?"
>
> Me: "All right, let's say your best friend's there."
>
> Austin: "And he jumps?"
>
> Me: "Yep, he jumps."
>
> Austin: "Is there a bear chasing me or something?"
>
> Me: "Sure, there's a big old bear right behind you."
>
> Austin: "And there's water below?"
>
> Me: "Yes."
>
> Austin: "How deep? Are we talking a shallow creek or a deep lake?"
>
> Me: "Oh, my goodness! Are you jumping or not? You can't grill me with all these questions. That's not the point here! It's not how the game works!"
>
> Austin: "Then what's the game about?"

Me: "It's an analogy that's supposed to show you that just because your friends do something doesn't mean you should blindly do it too without thinking it through."

Austin: "But I did think about it. That's why I asked about the bear and the water. Sometimes, you just don't make any sense, Mom!"

Austin's knack for diving deep into the details shouldn't have caught me off guard; it's just how he's wired. He sifts through life with an analytical lens, assessing the risks and rewards, always discerning to tilt the scales in favor of a wise decision. It's a trait I admire, even when it's used to challenge my mom-logic.

That episode with Austin was more than just a test of wills; it was a lesson to me, and now you, in navigating the murky waters of peer pressure and unsolicited advice. It was a reminder that our approach as parents should be as analytical and discerning as the minds we're molding, carefully evaluating the situation and asking the right questions before simply going along with what other parents might be doing.

Making Something Useful

Switching gears, let me walk you through a parallel that might not seem connected at first glance—the process of product development. This might sound like a leap, but stick with me.

In product development, the journey from a spark of an idea to a tangible item on the shelf is a meticulous one. It begins with identifying the passionate drivers, the visionaries, and the end users. (In mom world, it's like gathering your family and neighbors to decide on the best way to fix a common problem.)

First step in the process, they ask, "Who's really putting their heart into this?" It's all about pinpointing who cares the most: the folks dreaming it up, the team spreading the word, or the backers funding the dream. (For moms, the question sounds like, "Do these people have my back, or are they more like those sideline commentators with more opinions than practical help?")

Next, they get to the heart of the matter by asking these main folks, "What do we need to nail to make this thing a success?" This involves a bit of gathering and gabbing with those who have a stake in it, and maybe even creating a first draft version of the product. This prototype lets potential users test it out, giving the team a chance to see what works and what needs tweaking.

After they've rounded up a whole mess of feedback, it's time to sort through it, figuring out what's good or what's useless and irrelevant.

This is when the real heavy lifting starts when they need to sift through all that gathered wisdom to decide on the path forward. They look at what's crucial, anticipate any hitches, and brainstorm ways to smooth out any bumps. They're essentially asking, "What might go sideways if we pick this path?" and "How does this fit with the big picture we're aiming for?"

In the final stretch, they need to make a call on whether all the suggestions they've gathered line up with the project's true north. Is it practical? Does it serve the business, the product, and most importantly, the folks who'll end up using it? After all that pondering, they document their decisions, paving the way to bring their vision to life.

That's the long and short of how these folks in the business of making new things figure out the best path to turning a bright idea into something real and useful.

And look at that! You've just gotten a crash course in product engineering! But you might be scratching your head, wondering what all this has to do with the mountains of parenting advice we moms get thrown our way without even asking. Well, let me lay it out for you.

Imagine yourself as the engineer, handpicked by the grand architect of life itself, tasked with the monumental job of raising a tiny human. This little bundle, not shipped by any online store but given by the Creator, is your project, and only the Good Lord knows the ins and outs of how this is supposed to work out.

Long before we're ever handed our own, we dabble with the trial versions—other folks' kiddos. Whether it's through babysitting, helping out with our younger brothers and sisters, or playing the cool aunt with our nieces and nephews, we're getting our feet wet in the vast sea of parenthood.

And let's not forget about the Good Book and the solid ground of our community. They offer us guidelines and insights into the dos and don'ts of raising our little ones right. It's not that our circle of momma friends knows better than us, but there's something to be said about leaning on one another for support.

So, as the chief engineer in charge of this little life, it falls on you to sift through all that advice coming your way. Every single day, you're faced with decisions on how best to guide your little one to meet the expectations laid out by their teachers, future bosses, the family, and above all, aligning with what God has in store for them.

As moms, it's literally down to the nitty-gritty: analyzing. Which pieces of advice hold water? What aligns with your faith and family values, your parenting goals, and what's feasible? It's about prioritizing, assessing the impact, resolving any conflicts, and finally, deciding what's actually doable.

Y'all, navigating parenting advice can feel like trying to herd cats in a thunderstorm—messy, loud, and all over the place. You're gonna find yourself sorting through a whole heap of "shoulds" and "ought tos" from all corners—your family, the folks at church, even strangers at the grocery store. But here's the kicker: Amidst all that chatter, it's up to you to sift through and find the golden nuggets that actually fit your family.

You see, every single day, it's like you're piecing together a puzzle, picking up bits from one-on-one chats, and just observing how other families manage their rodeos. It's all about filtering that advice through a few key sieves: the heart behind it, who's dishing it out, and, most importantly, laying it all out in prayer to see if it's in line with God's playbook for your brood.

Now, should you come across a piece of advice that makes you pause and think, "Well, maybe there's something to this," that's when you roll up your sleeves and dive into it. It's about weighing that advice against your own family's compass and your values and asking, "Does this jive with what God is envisioning for my kiddos?"

This is where you have a heart-to-heart with the Man Upstairs, really pondering your family's mission statement. If the advice stands tall against your beliefs and what Scripture guides you toward, then you start wrestling with the what-ifs. How's this advice gonna play out in the daily dance of your family life? Could tweaking something for one kid create a domino effect for the others?

Encountering a hiccup along the way doesn't mean you chuck the whole idea. Sometimes, a little twist or turn to the advice can make it just right for your clan. It's about being steadfast in your core values while flexible enough to bend without breaking.

At the day's end, the big question is whether this piece of wisdom truly fits the bill for your household. Not all advice, no matter how shiny and well-intentioned, is gonna be the right fit for your here and now. Sometimes, a brilliant idea might just need to simmer on the back burner for a spell.

Charting Your Course

Mommas, all this sounds like a tall order, right? But hang tight because I've got another story about my son Austin that might just shine a light on how this whole process can unfold in real life.

Back in Austin's freshman year of high school, he found himself at a crossroads with football. Playing the game put him at a risk of injury that could sideline not just his season but also his dreams of wrestling in college, maybe even snagging a scholarship in something he's downright passionate about.

Austin's decision-making process was like a town hall meeting in his mind, weighing everyone's two cents. The football coach had his game plan, seeing Austin as a key player but not necessarily looking down the road at what Austin's dreams were and ultimate goals. Then there was us, his folks, fretting over his future and well-being. Austin himself was torn between the love of football and his overall aspirations.

Taking a step back, Austin laid out all the advice on the table, mulling over not just what the coach wanted or what we, his parents, were pushing for but what aligned with his own dreams and health. He realized that true friendship with his teammates didn't hinge on him risking it all on the football field.

After a good deal of soul-searching, Austin decided that stepping away from football was the right call. It wasn't an easy choice, mind you, but it was one that stayed true to the course God had set out for him. He knew deep down it was the best decision for safeguarding his future, even if it meant missing out on the immediate thrills of the game. A few years later, Austin recognized that he had made the wisest decision. Why? Because sticking to his dreams and goals paid off. (By the way, Austin did, indeed, sign with Colorado School of Mines).

And that, my friends, is the heart of it. When you're knee-deep in all sorts of advice, it's not just about sorting out what's good or what's useless and irrelevant based on what everyone else thinks. It's about lining everything up with your family's true north, guided by faith, and sometimes, that means taking the road less traveled to stay true to the path God's laid out for you and your loved ones.

We can't peek into what dreams or plans the Almighty has tucked away in our kid's hearts. But one thing's clearer than a spring morning: There's no love like what you've got for them. And you've been hand-picked by the Man Upstairs to provide everything they need to craft their chapter in His grand story.

Taking a lesson from Austin's playbook, our job isn't to dictate their dreams but to light the path so they can find their own way. It's like trying to write a story without knowing the last page. It's tricky, especially when we're not sure who'll play a part in their journey. Sure, we know they'll meet teachers, friends, love interests, and bump into all sorts of folks along the way, but the true measure of their impact only comes in hindsight.

Thankfully, the same hand that crafted the stars is guiding their steps. He's the one dialing in the updates and orchestrating meet-ups with just the right people to steer them straight.

Every day, a momma is faced with countless decisions, all in the name of guiding her little ones right. But even if you played a perfect game, is there really a recipe for the perfect child? I can almost hear the Lord chuckling at the thought. The truth is, there's no such thing as a perfect momma, but we do have a flawless Father above.

Let's not forget that even in the perfect Garden of Eden, things went sideways. And that first family? Well, their story tells us plenty about our knack for choosing the wrong path, even with the best of beginnings and the perfect environment.

Even our Father's first children stumbled—the ones who had unlimited access to Him. We can't expect a perfect track record. It's in those stumbles where the real learning happens. Our kids need to see us miss the mark now and then to learn the beauty of grace, growth, and forgiveness.

When you're sifting through unsolicited advice, measure it against what rings true to you and aligns with your faith, core values, and instincts. That way, even when things don't go as planned, you'll find peace in knowing you did your best with the cards you were dealt.

If you ever find yourself wondering if you've lost your way from the momma you aimed to be, you're not alone. We've all been there, wading through the sea of advice, trying to hold on to what matters most. It's worth taking a moment to think back on what guided you before the world started chipping in its two cents.

I encourage you to take a walk down memory lane, look back at the you from yesteryears, and see just how far you've come. Seeing your own growth can shine a light on the path forward, helping you navigate the ups and downs of motherhood with a bit more grace.

To find your true north again, strip back the layers of advice, even the bits that sting, till you uncover the heart of your own mothering style—the momma you've always aspired to be. Trust me, she's in there. I promise.

Trust your instincts and honor your feelings. Don't brush aside your gut or the emotions stirred by the advice you're given. Be open to change or to tweaking your course as you grow and learn from new experiences.

No matter where you are on this journey, your feelings are valid. Even when it feels like you're shouting into the void, remember you're heard by someone far greater. When the weight of your choices feels too heavy, remember, you're valued—by Him, by those who cherish you, and by me. He's rooting for you to find peace, to evolve into an even better version of yourself, inching ever closer to the purpose He's laid out for you.

Be kind to yourself as you sift through your thoughts and feelings. Allow yourself the freedom to adapt, embracing the lessons life throws your way. Admitting to a stumble can be tough, but don't miss out on the growth that comes from recognizing and moving past them.

If today doesn't look quite like you hoped, that's all right. Life's about finding your way, even when it means taking a detour. Think of it as a gentle course correction—a way to keep moving forward, learning, and growing stronger with each step.

Sure, the journey of motherhood is no cakewalk, but the rewards? They're richer than the most fertile soil. At the end of the day, isn't the goal to nurture these little ones until they're ready to spread their wings and soar?

The thought of letting them go might tug at your heartstrings, but it's part of the grand design. To help myself prepare, I got these little birdcage ornaments, one for each of my kiddos. As each one steps out into the world, I open them up, symbolizing their readiness to fly. It's a small gesture, but it helped me embrace the beauty of letting go.

It's tough, no doubt about it. They'll face their fair share of storms, but they need to chart their own course and grow into the people they're meant to be. And we'll always be there, cheering them on, loving them through every high and low.

And the best part? The rewards keep coming, even after they've left the nest. And if you're really lucky, you'll witness the joy—and maybe a bit of sweet revenge—when those grandbabies come along. Just sayin', y'all.

REFLECTIONS

Take it Straight to Jesus

Scripture Reading: Luke 8:43-48

> And there was a woman who had a discharge of blood for twelve years, and though she had spent all her living on physicians, she could not be healed by anyone. She came up behind him and touched the fringe of his garment, and immediately her discharge of blood ceased. And Jesus said, "Who was it that touched me?" When all denied it, Peter said, "Master, the crowds surround you and are pressing in on you!" But Jesus said, "Someone touched me, for I perceive that power has gone out from me." And when the woman saw that she was not hidden, she came trembling, and falling down before him declared in the presence of all the people why she had touched him, and how she had been immediately healed. And he said to her, "Daughter, your faith has made you well; go in peace."

In this story, we find a woman who had been sick and suffering for twelve long years. Twelve years, y'all! My heart hurts just knowing how I feel once a month, let alone her never-ending cycle for over a decade. I can't even!

She'd been round and round, seeking advice, pouring her heart and her money into finding a cure. The doctors she visited? Well, they didn't quite have her best interest at heart. They weren't the ones who knitted her together in her momma's womb, nor were they gonna be there at the end of her story.

What she really needed was a neon sign pointing straight to Jesus, the only one who could mend her from her constant bleeding. Despite following every piece of advice thrown her way, she found herself no better off. Yet, she didn't let go of hope; she clung to it, even through her suffering.

Imagine feeling so alienated from others who viewed her as unclean. This left her always on the outside looking in.

But when she finally laid her troubles at Jesus' feet—well, that's when everything changed. He didn't just heal her; He did it in such a way that everyone around could see. He called her out, not to embarrass her, but to show her she was seen, valued, and had a place in His story—all because of her faith. Jesus asked, "Who touched me?" not because He didn't know but to give her a moment to stand up and be recognized for her faith. It was her moment of claiming that faith openly, a public declaration that she needed Him. And that wasn't just for her sake but for all those watching to see and believe for themselves.

It was like Jesus was giving advice without saying a word (let that one sink in), letting everyone around witness this miracle and think, "Maybe I ought to put my trust in Him too." With the crowd as witnesses, the truth of what happened was as solid as the ground underfoot. It was undeniable.

Now, we all go through times when we're seeking advice, trying to figure things out, maybe even looking to news articles or the latest trends for answers. But at the end of the day, it's where that advice is coming from that matters. It's got to be rooted in something solid, something true—like the Good Book.

We might not have an instruction manual for every little thing in life, especially when it comes to raising our little ones, but we've got the Bible. And sometimes, it's about trusting our gut and the guidance of those around us, all the while holding tight to what we know deep down to be true and right.

So, are we focused on the right source, the one that leads to the best outcome? Or are we spinning in circles and wasting time and resources in a never-ending cycle without ever really solving a problem or finding the right solution—like the woman who suffered for twelve years before finally encountering Jesus?

God's Word is steadfast, always there to guide us. Walking by faith means trusting in His Word, knowing it's never empty or lacking in what we need.

As we sift through all the advice and opinions out there, it's crucial to think about who we're listening to and why. Are we turning to the right place for wisdom? Any change or growth we go through, any advice we take in, ought to leave us better than before. If it doesn't lift us up, why hold on to it?

It's about finding freedom in the truth, letting go of what weighs us down, and stepping into the life God's got mapped out for us. True advice, the kind that comes from above, sets us free to live the life we're meant to live, especially as moms doing our best to guide our little ones on the right path.

Consider this message your neon sign pointing you to Jesus and His Word for whatever ails you today and for whatever problems you are facing. Guidance, comfort, wisdom, hope, assurance, peace, answers, and so much more are just a fingertip and Bible flip away.

Just like Jesus wanted to spotlight the woman and her faith for others to witness, you, too, have the opportunity to spotlight your faith with your little ones watching.

What a wonderful opportunity and mission field!

Moms, you have an incredible calling and a field that will yield exponential rewards, seen and unseen, in the years ahead. You've got this!

Prayer

Heavenly Father,

Thank You for the beautiful, messy, and sacred journey of motherhood. In the whirlwind of advice, opinions, and expectations, help us to pause, breathe, and fix our eyes on You—the true source of wisdom and peace. Teach us to sift through the noise with discernment, to hold fast to what is good, and to let go of what doesn't align with the values and purpose You've placed in our hearts.

Like the woman who reached out to touch the hem of Jesus' garment, may we boldly bring our questions, doubts, and burdens straight to You. Remind us that You see us, know us, and call us "daughter," not because of our perfection but because of our faith. When we feel unseen or overwhelmed, whisper Your truth to our hearts—that we are enough, not because of what we do, but because of who we are in You.

Give us the courage to parent not from fear or comparison, but from a place of faith, trusting that You have uniquely equipped us to guide and nurture the children You've entrusted to us. Help us model grace, resilience, and unwavering trust in You, even when we stumble. And when we do, remind us that Your mercies are new every morning.

Bless the hearts of every mother reading these words. Strengthen her where she feels weak, comfort her where she feels uncertain, and fill her with the peace that surpasses all understanding. May her heart always return to You, the One who lovingly crafted her and holds both her and her children in the palm of Your hand.

In Jesus' name,

Amen.

Small Group Discussion Questions

1. In your opinion, why is it important for parents to critically evaluate unsolicited parenting advice rather than blindly following it?
2. Can you share any examples where blindly following such advice had negative consequences?
3. How can parents strike a balance between being open to new ideas and suggestions while also maintaining their own values and parenting style?
4. What strategies can help navigate conflicting advice?
5. What role does parental intuition or instinct play in your decision-making? How might the process of evaluating advice contribute to personal growth and parenting skills?

Self-Care Affirmations

- I trust my instincts as a parent and use them as a valuable guide in evaluating unsolicited parenting advice.

- I am open-minded and willing to consider different perspectives.

- I am the expert on my own children and can discern what is best for them.

- I value the input and experiences of others, but I have the power to filter and evaluate unsolicited advice, taking only what aligns with my values and parenting style.

- I am confident in my ability to make informed decisions for my children, weighing the advice I receive against my own knowledge and research.

- I appreciate the intentions behind unsolicited parenting advice, recognizing that it often comes from a place of care and concern, but I am empowered to decide what is ultimately best for my family.

CHAPTER FIVE

RESPONDING TO UNSOLICITED ADVICE

Who doesn't love a good comeback? I've tucked away some gems over the years, so here are a few polished and kind-hearted comebacks to keep up your sleeve for those unexpected moments of unsolicited parenting wisdom:

> "I truly value your concern for our family. We're content with our approach, but thank you."

> "Thanks for your insight. I'll consider it."

> "That's an interesting perspective. I hadn't thought about it that way. I appreciate you sharing."

> "Would you listen to that? My dogs seem to be summoning me. Must dash, but let's chat more later!"

At times, the art of silence speaks volumes. Just lend an ear until the conversation naturally shifts to another topic.

Let me paint you a picture of a day I'll never erase from my memory. Ethan, our youngest son, was navigating some rough waters with his behavior in kindergarten at his private Christian school. One particular day, he found himself on a solo mission to the principal's office. As he perched outside her door, he spied an escape route to freedom through an inadvertently open door. Seizing the moment, Ethan made a dash for it, sending the school into an uproar and us, his parents, into a meeting we'd never anticipated, joining our son for a cozy little chat with the school principal.

My knee-jerk reaction? To leap to our defense and Ethan's. It's a tough pill to swallow, realizing your child might be facing challenges. However, I listened to the principal's concerns, including Ethan's sensory issues, impulse control, and outbursts.

It doesn't get more personal than receiving advice about your child's well-being, even when the feedback comes from a knowledgeable, well-meaning expert. I listened because we all wanted to help Ethan flourish, and I am grateful for their wisdom, insight, and expertise. I'm happy to report that I welcomed their advice about my son with open ears, even though every ounce of me was closed off initially. It's not always that easy. I lent my ear because we all shared the same dream: to see Ethan thrive. Their knowledge and insight were gifts, and embracing their suggestions with an open heart wasn't simple, but it was necessary.

Following the principal's guidance, my husband Luke and I introduced Ethan to a program aimed at equipping him for a triumphant start to first grade. And guess what? He nailed it! Ethan crushed every program goal and passed with flying colors!

When Ethan wrapped up his program—where he basically aced it—the school's call for a meeting had me thinking, "Next steps? We're all in. My boy's on a roll! He's kicking it!"

But sometimes, life throws a curveball. Have you ever walked into a meeting with all confidence and smiles, expecting it to go a certain way, but when people start talking, you begin to wonder if you're in the wrong room? "Surely, they're not talking about our kid" was exactly what I was thinking.

Suddenly, the puzzle pieces started to fall into place, and it was much different than the picture Luke and I had painted before we walked in. What we thought would happen in the meeting, well, didn't. In fact, just the opposite.

In the end, the school nurse brought to light additional concerns beyond Ethan's ongoing battles with impulse control. She pointed out that Ethan seemed too small, too short, and emotionally unprepared for the leap to first grade. Her verdict? Another round of kindergarten was "best for him."

We were taken aback, and the news literally sucked the air out of me. After a summer of diligently following our plan and witnessing Ethan's growth and triumphs, it felt like a huge setback. New hurdles were being tossed at us—over which none of us had any control.

My response? "I don't think so!"

What would you say, and how would you respond in this situation? I know how I responded—and it wasn't pretty! I took it very personally.

I was seething on the inside, silent but storming. Sure, I sat quietly, but the thunder rolled! Well, two can play at this game, I thought. The nurse had a laundry list of criticisms about my son, prompting me to silently draft my own list of her shortcomings.

While she told me why my baby boy couldn't go to first grade, I made a mental checklist of the reasons why she was unqualified to make such a decision.

Starting with her hairstyle.

If a grown woman can't figure out how to use a hair dryer, she's got no business running my kid's life.

Then there was the way she pronounced her Rs. The next one up for therapy is you, Lady!

And worst of all was that smile! Just no. A definite no-go!

Bad hairdo—check!

Can't enunciate—check, *check*!

Crooked smile—check, *check*, CHECK!

As my list grew, so did my anger. Even as I prayed, "Oh, Lord, help me," in my mind, I was gloved up, circling the ropes, and ready to rumble. It took everything in me not to slam my hands on the desk and yell, "Oh, yeah! Well, I'm short, too, but I bet I can take you!"

My husband Luke can read me like a book, and he knows that a silent Andrea is a woman about to erupt. And just when I was about to pounce, he caught my eye and cautiously but gently touched my arm—a risky move at such a moment! Y'all, he's lucky to still have his arm! Poor man.

I prayed even harder for my heart to remain open. I needed Jesus to take the wheel, give me guidance, and show me the answers we needed for Ethan. All I know is that by the end of the meeting, we officially agreed to disagree.

About three weeks later, the little fighter in me finally stepped out of the ring and put the gloves away. Without her taking jabs at my sanity, I could open my heart to acknowledge a few possible, somewhat valid points of concern.

Luke and I eventually did some research and talked to our pediatrician. We decided to help boost Ethan's confidence by transferring him to a new school with more resources to guide his long-term success.

Switching schools was a logistical challenge, especially since it meant moving all our children out of private education. We fretted over how Ethan and Cameron would adapt, but the change proved to be a blessing in disguise.

The bigger school opened a whole new world for my entire family. Where Ethan had struggled at his old school, now he flourished and overcame his challenges. In fact, the new school had better funding and more resources to help all my kids thrive. A larger population also meant more friends, and Luke and I made wonderful connections as well. Not only did we meet parents going through similar struggles, but my whole family formed precious friendships.

I certainly could have responded better to the nurse's recommendation when Ethan was in kindergarten. Her advice wasn't totally wrong; Ethan did need more help. But I'm glad that we paused to ask what type of help he needed instead of following one person's advice without question.

I admit it took a long, hot minute to move through the initial shock, but I eventually got there. Finally, with open ears, I could hear what the nurse had to say. I could think clearly, navigate the unexpected plot twists, and follow God's plan for our lives.

Throughout my motherhood journey, God has given me many opportunities to learn a very important lesson: The best way to receive advice is with open ears, a lot of grace, a grain of salt, and, sometimes, with a trusted source's gentle hand on your arm to help guide you.

When to Respond with Open Ears

Let's talk about the art of listening—truly listening. It's a bit like sitting on the porch swing on a slow summer evening, letting the words float around you like fireflies before you decide to catch them in your jar. I've come to learn the grace in holding my tongue, letting those hard-to-swallow words settle in my mind before I let my own spill out. It's about giving those words, the ones that might prick like a thorn, a chance to bloom into something worth pondering.

Now, back in chapter two, we strolled down the path of understanding those folks who offer up their nuggets of wisdom with nothing but love in their hearts. They're like the neighbor who brings over a homemade pie, not expecting anything in return but a smile. They lay out their experiences as raw and real as they come, knowing full well they might get a side-eye or two. But bless their hearts; their intention is as pure as spring water—they're just trying to light the way for another soul on this winding path of parenthood.

When you find yourself on the receiving end of such golden-hearted advice, why not respond with a curiosity as deep as the roots of an old oak tree? Ask them to unfold their tale a bit more and to share the chapters you haven't heard yet. It's like offering them a seat at your kitchen table, where the real stories come out over cups of coffee. This does a little two-step with the conversation—it twirls it away from just stewing over the problem to rolling up your sleeves and tackling it together.

But here's a spoonful of wisdom to keep in your apron pocket: Sometimes, the tales folks share are borrowed from someone else's book. They might only know a snippet—a scene out of a much bigger story—and they pass it along to you like a hand-me-down quilt. It's okay to fold up that second-hand advice and tuck it away in your hope chest for another day. It might just be the patchwork piece you need down the line.

Now, for those moments when you're sifting through advice, wondering if there's a nugget of truth for your journey, here are a few questions that might just help you pan for gold:

Find out if their situation is similar to yours:

- What is your story?
- What led you to think of this?
- Can I ask you to tell me more about your own circumstances?
- Why did you implement that?

Find out where the advice came from:

- Did you read a book or watch a show about that?
- Did your doctor tell you that?
- Where does that information come from?
- Is there a website where I can learn more?
- Are you part of a group that provides information?

Find out how they implemented the advice:

- How long did it take to change that behavior?
- What challenges did you find in the transition?
- How did it impact other family members?

Find out the result:

- How did that work for your child?
- How did that change your family's life?
- How did that give you more peace or structure?
- Do you feel like your household runs smoother?
- Are you less stressed from implementing these things?

Sometimes, those nuggets of wisdom will come from women I like to call connectors. You know—it's those moms who share their advice and their own stories of struggle because they're looking for validation, understanding, and a personal connection.

The Bible lays it out plain as day, telling us, "Bear one another's burdens, and so fulfill the law of Christ" (Galatians 6:2). Reaching out to share and work through our troubles together isn't just something that feels right in our hearts; it's downright biblical. We're called upon to offer up our prayers and lend a helping hand through those rough patches.

That verse doesn't stop there, though. It goes on to remind us that standing by each other isn't merely a friendly suggestion; it's part and parcel of living by God's commandments. The very essence of Christ's teaching is to love your neighbor as much as you love yourself. So when someone comes to you, heart in hand, sharing their journey, offering them a kind word isn't just nice—it's essential.

But, momma, there's a whole lot more to it than just doing as we're told. Everything the Lord guides us to do is meant to lift us up, to make us better. When you take a moment to support another momma, you're stepping into a role God's crafted just for you, acting as a vessel of His peace and comfort. It takes a heap of courage to open up, sharing both the pain and the wisdom that comes with it. By greeting their advice with a heart full of kindness, you turn into a living, breathing answer to their prayers.

So, let's remember to approach one another's stories with a listening ear and a gentle heart, ready to offer encouragement or a shoulder to lean on. It's not just about following rules; it's about filling our days with acts of love and kindness, being there for each other in the same way we hope someone will be there for us. In this great big family of ours, being a source of comfort and a beacon of hope to one another is one of the most beautiful ways we can live out our faith.

This journey of mine has taught me that kindness and understanding flow both ways. When folks take a moment to care about how you're holding up, the gracious thing to do is to listen with all you've got, to soak in their wisdom, and to show your thanks. This not only helps us grow but also stitches us closer together in the quilt of community.

So, I'm nudging you to lean into conversations with open hearts. Listen to those connectors with ears wide open. Starting from a stance of genuine acceptance gears you up to either cherish the wisdom shared from a generous heart or to be the comfort a weary and hurting mom might just be praying for. In doing so, we don't just enrich our own lives but weave stronger bonds in the tapestry of our shared mothering journey, guided by the light of love and understanding that shines from above.

When to Respond with Grace

Now, let's sit a spell and ponder on a bit of a prickly patch—handling those who dish out what feels like unsolicited advice with a side of sour—those dirty diaper dealers.

There's a tale, kind of like one of those fables your grandma might've told you, about a donkey, a tiger, and a lion that might just shed some light on this predicament.

Once upon a time, in a land where critters could chat, a donkey got it into his head that the grass was blue. He told the tiger so, sparking a bit of a barnyard brouhaha. "Nonsense," the tiger said, "Everyone knows the grass is green!" They bickered back and forth until they decided to lay the matter before the lion, the jungle's king and judge.

Marching up to the lion's throne, the donkey hollered, "Your Majesty, isn't it true the grass is blue?" The lion, with the patience of a saint, replied, "If you believe it's so, then yes, the grass is blue for you." The donkey, not missing a beat, demanded, "The tiger's been arguing, saying I'm wrong. Can you believe that? Punish him!"

So, the lion decreed the tiger would be silent for three days. The donkey danced a jig, hollering, "The grass is blue!" The tiger, bewildered, asked the lion, "Why am I being punished when we both know the grass is green?" The lion shared a nugget of wisdom, "This punishment isn't about the color of the grass, but about why a creature as noble as you would waste time arguing with a donkey, and worse, drag me into this mess."

The moral here? Arguing with someone who's set in their ways, who cares more for their pride than the truth, is like trying to teach a pig to sing; it wastes your time and annoys the pig. When ignorance is loud, wisdom knows when to walk away.

Just like the tiger, we sometimes don't know when to call it quits. Recognizing when an argument is going nowhere is a skill. Knowing when to bow out gracefully without ruffling feathers or regretting words left hanging in the air requires wisdom. Lord knows, there have been times I've wished for a mute button, especially when my thoughts decide to parade around without my permission.

And what about those moments when you spot a loose thread on your brand-new shirt? You pull it, right? Sometimes, it snaps off clean, but other times, you end up unraveling the whole darn sleeve, leaving you in a pickle. Sometimes, the need to be right is like that. Standing your ground, insisting you're right, can sometimes unravel more than you bargained for.

As we keep talking, the situation continues to unravel, exposing more of you than anyone wanted to see. When nothing you say is going to make a difference, it's time to stop talking. You don't want to shut down your voice, but sometimes silence says more.

Every workplace has that armchair physician lurking in the elevators who needs to have the last word. If their insistence is persistent, you need to recognize when they are just trying to suck you into their crazy. Go ahead and let them believe your doctor is stupid, you're giving birth to sextuplets next week, and the grass is blue.

We all know those voices, clamoring for our attention, vying for the "World's Best Mom" trophy. But in truth, they've strayed from their path, forgetting that their real job is to be the best parent they can be to their own little ones. We need to peel back the intention behind their words, preserve our peace, and keep our focus where it truly belongs.

Listening for that whisper of discernment from above can guide us through these moments of folly. And if you find yourself face-to-face with a donkey munching on "blue grass," maybe try responding with a gentle deflection and a nod to their story. Then, try a swift change of subject or a graceful exit. Something like:

- "I'll mull that over, thank you kindly. By the way, do you know where the nearest restroom is?"
- "That's interesting, and I'm glad it worked for you. I'm off to run some errands now, but it was nice catching up!"
- "Thanks for sharing that. I'll chat about it with my spouse. So, what's the latest you've been bingeing on Netflix?"

Navigating these encounters with a mix of grace, wisdom, and a touch of humor can turn even the most awkward moments into just another part of this wild ride we call life.

When to Respond with a Grain of Salt

The other day, I found myself chuckling over a sight at a local diner—a little fella, no bigger than a minute, was shoving his highchair away from the table with all the might his tiny arms could muster. It was as if he was declaring, "I don't know who these folks are, but I've had my fill of 'em. I'm outta here. Adios!" It got me wondering, who in tarnation thought it was a bright idea to give these escape pods, aka highchairs, a set of wheels? Sure, it's handy for scooting across the kitchen, but it strikes me as a bit of a head-scratcher. If we're going to equip these kiddos with wheels, shouldn't we at least have the sense to throw in some brakes?

This got me thinking about how we all handle advice, much like that determined tot wanting to make a getaway. Advice, depending on our walk of life, hits us all a bit differently, shaping the way we sift and sort through what's tossed our way. There are times, just like that baby, when we find ourselves wanting to put as much distance as possible between us and the well-meaning folks trying to spoon-feed us their two cents.

We might not say a word, but inside, we're thinking, "Thanks, but no thanks. I've got this."

Sometimes, the advice we're given just doesn't fit the bill. Maybe we gave it a whirl once, and it flopped. Or perhaps a snippet of what was said intertwines with a bit from someone else, and down the line, a spark from a blog or a snippet from a commercial lights up an idea, making us reconsider. Our circumstances might have shifted, making room for that advice to take root in new soil.

So, next time you find yourself on the receiving end of advice that feels about as fitting as a square peg in a round hole, just remember that diner scene. Sometimes, all you can do is smile, nod, and, in your best toddler-on-the-run impression, scoot away—no brakes needed.

Then there are moments when advice grates on us like nails on a chalkboard, and we're mentally high-tailing it out of there, no brakes on our highchair, saying, "See ya!" It's like we're all toddlers at heart, ready to bolt at the first sign of unsolicited wisdom.

And let's not forget about those pearls of advice so far-fetched they might as well be from another planet. In those instances, we take it all with a pinch of salt, knowing full well that not every piece of advice is worth its weight in gold. It's all about finding the balance—taking in what could serve us well and learning when to just breathe, offer up a prayer, and keep our peace.

Always Embrace God's Plan

Even in those moments when my spirit is itching for a fight and my knees are about as stable as a newborn calf, I find the strength to fold my hands and pray. It's a powerful truth, y'all: God understands the stirrings of our hearts, even when our reactions might suggest we're about ready to kick up a dust storm. No matter how many folks we listen to or how meticulously we lay our plans, life has a way of nudging us down paths we never saw coming. But here's the thing—it's all part of His grand design.

Believe it or not, most folks doling out advice are doing so with the best of intentions. It's worth keeping that in your heart, even when their words might land like a June bug at a garden party. Sure, some folks could stand to sweeten their delivery, and yeah, there'll be times when the criticism is heavy. But I promise you, there's light on the other side of that thicket.

When advice grates on us, it can stick like burrs on a wool sock. Don't let yourself be so weighed down by what others think that you lose sight of the path God's laid out for you and your little ones. No matter how you react to the guidance thrown your way, the Lord is busy weaving His purpose behind the scenes.

Life can sometimes feel like you're trying to herd cats in a tornado. You find yourself wondering, "What in the world does all this mean? How's any good supposed to come from this mess?" There might be a sliver, a single thread you can tease out from the tangle that helps make sense of the journey you're on.

A young man once asked me, "How do you know God's really there?" Well, there've been times, I'll admit, when feeling His presence was about as likely as catching fog in a mason jar. But then, there are those moments when His touch is as real as the summer sun on your face, as comforting as a hand resting gently on your heart.

In those seasons when God seems as distant as the far side of the moon, that's when we need to walk by the faith we've placed in Jesus. It does get easier, momma. His plan will unfold, as unfailing as the dawn, because nothing and no one can steer His purpose off course—not for our lives, and not for our children's.

Even when the road map is a mystery, we can stride forward with confidence because Romans 8:28 gives us this promise: "And we know that for those who love God all things work together for good." That "good" might not always be what we had in mind. Sometimes, what we go through is meant to be a blessing to someone else, a concept that sure can be hard to wrap our heads around. But we can rest assured every bit of it serves His greater plan. Our trials—they're not for naught.

It's tough, no doubt, to see the silver lining when you're walking through a storm. Yet it's often through the toughest times that the most profound blessings emerge. Every twist and turn in our journey unfurls something new, something beautiful. Recognizing the intricate way all these threads come together, creating the tapestry of our lives, that's a sight to behold.

It might take a spell, but eventually, we come to understand we won't see the end of the road while we're still on the journey. We're living out just a chapter of a much grander story, unable to see how all the pieces fit. That's okay. We don't need all the answers before we take the first step. Along the way, we carry with us dreams we've cherished and hopes we've nurtured. But then, out of the blue, we're showered with blessings we never even dared to imagine.

It's all too easy to lose sight of the gifts God has planted in our hands for this journey called motherhood. Yes, it's hard work, but with His strength, you can do it. He chose you to be the momma to your children, equipping you uniquely for the task. He didn't give you the strength to raise someone else's kids, nor did He give another woman the tools your kids need. Remember, you've got to be you—because I'm already taken.

REFLECTIONS

Listening to Bad Advice: Lessons from Job

Scripture Reading: Job 2:11-13, 4:7-9, and 38:1-2

We've established that we're often faced with unsolicited advice from well-meaning friends, family, and even strangers. Sometimes, this advice can be helpful, but other times, it can be misguided or even harmful. Let's draw wisdom from the story of Job and learn how to handle such situations with grace and discernment.

Job was a man who faced unimaginable suffering, and in his darkest moments, his friends came to offer advice. Initially, they sat with him in silence, empathizing with his pain (Job 2:11-13). However, when they began to speak, their words were filled with assumptions and accusations rather than comfort and wisdom.

Eliphaz, one of Job's friends, was the first to speak. He suggested that Job's suffering must be a result of his own sin (Job 4:7-9). This advice was not only incorrect but also deeply hurtful. Instead of bringing comfort, it added to Job's distress.

In the end, God Himself responded to Job and his friends, making it clear that their understanding was flawed. He said, "Who is this that darkens counsel by words without knowledge?" (Job 38:1-2). God corrected their misconceptions and restored Job's fortunes, demonstrating His sovereignty and justice.

Lessons for Moms

As mommas, we often encounter advice from others regarding our parenting choices. Some advice can be like Eliphaz's—misguided and hurtful, based on incomplete understanding.

Here are some takeaways and lessons we can learn from Job's experience:

Discernment is Key: Not all advice is created equal. Just as Job had to discern the truth in his friends' words, we need to filter advice through the lens of our own values and circumstances. "The wisdom of the prudent is to discern his way, but the folly of fools is deceiving" (Proverbs 14:8).

Respond with Grace: When receiving unsolicited advice, it's important to respond with grace. Job's friends had good intentions, but their delivery was flawed. We can choose to respond with kind-hearted comebacks, acknowledging the intent behind the advice even if we don't agree with it. "A soft answer turns away wrath, but a harsh word stirs up anger" (Proverbs 15:1).

Seek God's Guidance: Above all, seek God's guidance in all things. When we are unsure, we can pray for wisdom and discernment. "If any of you lacks wisdom, let him ask of God, who gives generously to all without reproach, and it will be given him" (James 1:5).

Application

Reflecting on the story about Ethan and the challenges faced with his behavior and schooling, we see a real-life parallel to Job's experience. Just as Job had to navigate through bad advice, so do we as parents. When Ethan's school nurse suggested holding him back, my initial reaction was defensive. However, through prayer, reflection, and open ears, a better path was found for Ethan that led to unexpected blessings.

Just as Job navigated through the bad advice of his friends with faith and patience, we, too, can handle unsolicited parenting advice with grace, discernment, and trust in God's guidance. Let's embrace the journey with confidence, knowing that God equips us uniquely for the task of raising our children.

Prayer

Dear Heavenly Father, thank You for the wisdom found in Your Word. Help us to discern good advice from bad and to respond with grace and kindness. Guide us in our parenting journey, and give us the strength to follow Your plan for our families.

In Jesus' name,

Amen.

Small Group Discussion Questions

1. Considering "connectors," who share from a place of vulnerability and seek validation, how can we foster a supportive environment for sharing difficult stories, in line with the biblical encouragement to bear each other's burdens?
2. Balancing others' wisdom with God's unique plan for us can be challenging. How do you navigate this, especially regarding advice on parenting and personal decisions?
3. Can you share a time when life felt chaotic and purposeless, only to later recognize God's positive intervention in hindsight?
4. In moments when God's presence feels distant, how has your faith been tested, and what strategies have supported your continued trust in His plan?

5. The journey of life is a tapestry of experiences, advice, and challenges. Can you share a personal anecdote when you've seen these elements intertwine, contributing to growth or positively impacting others?

Self-Care Affirmations

- I embrace the wisdom shared by others, filtering it through God's plan for me and finding the gems meant for my path.
- I am a beacon of kindness and understanding, responding to others' vulnerabilities with compassion that mirrors God's love.
- I hold the power to discern, choosing wisely which advice lights my way and which to let pass like leaves on a stream.
- I am not swayed by the storm of unsolicited advice, for I stand firm in the knowledge of my unique purpose and God's promises.
- I find strength in silence, recognizing when to let go of fruitless debates and when to embrace peace over proving a point.
- I see the tapestry of my life unfolding, each thread of experience, advice, and challenge woven by God's hand into a masterpiece.
- I am resilient, turning trials into testimonies and understanding that sometimes the good that comes from challenges is meant to uplift others.

CHAPTER SIX

DEALING WITH PERSISTENT UNSOLICITED PARENTING ADVICE

Recently, my daughter had a few tough days during her monthly cycle. As she was venting her frustration, she joked, "When I get to heaven, me and Eve, we're gonna have words! There's gonna be some throwing hands with that woman!"

We all have ideas about how we think the world should work, and our kids are no exception. All my favorite parenting advice comes from my kids. It usually starts with something like, "Well, my friends Lexi, Tyler, and Marissa all have iPhone 23 X-Max Pro, and they are all allowed to play games until midnight every Monday, so I should too!"

My standard response (after the jumping-off-the-bridge interrogation with Austin) is, "I am sorry, but I didn't give birth to those kids, so I really don't care what their parents say. You obey my rules. And when you're over there, you can follow their rules as long as it doesn't go against our morals."

I just shake my head because they have no clue. But aren't we all a little like that? We all have our list of questions and suggestions for

God, and I think Eve is at the top of most of our lists. And I imagine God is up there chuckling, "Oh, you're so cute. I can't wait till you get here so I can tell you why you have no idea."

Whether it's with our kids, our friends and family, total strangers, or even God, we all have moments when we just don't know when to drop it, and we take it too far. That's what this chapter is about—how to deal with persistent unsolicited advice from people who keep coming back to tell you how to do it better.

As my parents have gotten older, I've found myself promoted to the honorary role of family chauffeur, shepherding my aging parents through their golden years. Their handicap sticker became a semi-permanent fixture in my car this past year, a silent witness to our journeys. These rides, cherished by Mom and Dad, offer us many confined moments together—some of which I secretly treasure.

Then there are my favorite moments with my dad, when he morphs into the sage of the highway, transforming "Andrea's Uber" into a classroom on wheels. No sooner does he click his seatbelt than we're transported to a realm where he's the maestro of maneuvering. "Turn here—not so fast! That stop sign wasn't a suggestion. Look out for that truck! Was that light really yellow?"

Thirty years behind the wheel, and yet, in these moments, I'm a novice once again. There I sit, smile plastered on, entertaining thoughts of dramatic escape. "How fun would it be if I suddenly braked for a phantom squirrel?" Or better yet, "How much would it set me back to install an ejector seat, just like Batman's? I'd make sure the parachute gently deposits my dad in my sister's backyard—what a grand entrance that would be."

While situations like this can try my patience, it's harmless, and I'm sure I'll do the same to my kids someday. But it's not always just about cheekily weathering Dad's backseat driving. There's a delicate dance of honoring his words while guarding my own space. When advice veers off my path, I find safety in responses like, "Got it, thanks," or "I'll roll that thought around a bit."

Then there are those times when dealing with the foundations of your being—your parents—becomes a complex ballet of emotions and respect. Allow me one more tale from the chronicles of being forever Daddy's girl for those of us who wear that title like a badge of honor.

Our oldest son, Cameron, was four years old when he served as the ring bearer in my sister's wedding. He was so handsome in his little tuxedo, and I couldn't wait for the pictures. However, getting the pictures was a bit of a challenge.

It had been a long day for both young and old by the time the photographer called the wedding party. My dad was exhausted and stressed, and Cameron was tired and fidgety. When Cameron struggled to follow directions and sit still, Dad had a moment.

Don't get me wrong, my dad is a wonderful grandpa. But in that moment, he was spent. This time, his response was more than acting as a backseat driver. He swerved into my parenting lane a little too much, and I couldn't just look the other way. At the same time, he's my father, and I love him.

I pulled him aside and quietly said, "Dad, that was unnecessary. He's four. You know you can discipline him when I'm not around, but I'm right here in the room. If he gets out of line, I will take care of him."

We know it takes a village to raise a child, and it's usually those who have been in your life forever who have the most liberties in helping you raise your kids. Therefore, when emotions are high (or sleep is low), they are also the most likely to step over your boundaries. When they do, you must make a choice to either lash out, hold your tongue, or have a respectful conversation.

Enforcing boundaries respectfully takes balance, but I'd estimate you'll be able to do it about ninety percent of the time. But, if you're like me, you'll lose your temper the other ten percent! You won't always have the presence of mind to reinforce your boundaries so that the relationship can move forward in a healthy way.

Sometimes, things just happen. There will be days you are so overwhelmed, exhausted, and stressed that it blows up in your face, and you will wish for a do-over.

Some of the advice you get will launch over that fence line like a hot dog launcher at a baseball game. It's like an incoming dirty diaper that flies through your filters during a moment of weakness.

If you don't have clear boundaries in your life, you won't know how to protect yourself from those dirty diaper dealers. Dirty diapers can come out of nowhere and smack you right in the nose, just like when you played dodgeball on the playground.

In dodgeball, if you don't get out of the way, you get hit, and it just lights you up. You fall on the floor with a hot, red welt on your face or a stinging bruise on your arm. Those are the immediate, tangible, and powerful outcomes of making a wrong move or getting in someone's way. The hurt and embarrassment are a special kind of consequence, and you think, "Oh, I don't want that to happen again."

You are going to get hit; you are going to get knocked down. You have to pick yourself up off the floor and re-engage in the game. You change your patterns. You learn who to avoid, when to duck, and when you just gotta pivot so that they hit more cushioned parts of the body. You learn to minimize the damage.

It's no different when dealing with persistent advice. When a dirty diaper bomb lands —BAM!!—sometimes you have no idea what just happened. You don't catch it in time, your diaper-handling skills fail, and it splats face-down on the floor. Now what?

You get out the heavy-duty disinfectants and high-power air purifiers, clean it up, take out the trash, wash your hands, and move on.

I promise those dirty diapers are gonna get you. In fact, you have to take a hit occasionally if you're going to stay humble. What do you do when your boundaries are crossed, you don't handle it as well as you could have, and now there's a mess left behind?

You know your boundary has been crossed when you sense that burning hint of betrayal, and it stops you for a moment. You process through the failure and the hurt. Then you'll get back up and do the damage control through hard conversations, apologies, and shared tears. You may even take a hit to the bank account once or twice.

But once the mess is clean and you've washed your hands, you think, "Boy, I don't ever want to have to go through that again." And you can move on better for the growth and with newfound knowledge for how to reinforce your boundaries.

Enforcing boundaries gets easier as you have more experience. People will never stop throwing dirty diapers, so you'll get plenty of practice and chances to get things right. As you go through icky situations, you grow, and your boundaries become more stable.

Over time, you realize what influences and advice do not belong in your life, and you learn to recognize red flags. Then you can say, "I'm out of here. I'm not going to deal with that."

Every time you realize a particular piece of advice doesn't work for your family or your kids—that's a new boundary.

You might hear someone speak in a way that contradicts your core and think, "Well, it's probably harmless." But wait! You've heard things like this before, and it didn't end well.

We get anxious when something doesn't feel right and our boundaries are compromised. It's easy to second-guess yourself and feel unsteady in what you're doing. How you handle those intrusions depends on who you're dealing with. You may be direct when someone outside your bedrock is getting into your business. This could be a clear admonition such as, "You don't know my child well enough to give me advice right now. Please let me handle this."

However, there's more opportunity to make a mess when someone in your bedrock goes too far. We all make mistakes. If you're willing to grow and learn, people will understand. Enforcing boundaries is hard. It takes work and practice to learn and grow through the experience. Give yourself grace through the process.

I have learned how to handle these circumstances better by following a process of discovering my core and my purpose to guide what input I will accept and what I will decline. For you, too, it's about discovering your unwavering "Yes" amidst a sea of opinions and being clear on your "No," especially when the advice feels as persistent as a summer mosquito buzzing in your ear.

So, how do we embark on this voyage of self-discovery, ensuring that our parenting compass points true north? Let's dive into the steps to uncover your steadfast "Yes" and your firm "No."

Discovering Your "Yes"

Reflect on Your Values

1. The cornerstone of your "Yes" lies in what you hold dear. Is it independence, empathy, or resilience? Identifying these values helps sift through the noise, embracing advice that amplifies these virtues in your parenting.

Seek Inspiration, Not Instruction

2. Look to those you admire—not for a rulebook on parenting but for inspiration. Let their wisdom ignite your intuition, guiding your unique path.

Embrace Your Child's Individuality

3. Your "Yes" should resonate with the unique spirit of your child. What works for one may not for another. Tailor your acceptance of advice based on what nurtures your child's growth and happiness.

Knowing Your "No"

Trust Your Gut

4. Often, your instinct whispers your "No" before your mind catches up. If advice doesn't sit well with your gut, it's likely not right for your family. Trust that inner voice.

Educate Yourself

5. Knowledge is power. The more you understand about child development and parenting philosophies, the clearer your "No" becomes. This doesn't mean becoming rigid but informed.

Establish Boundaries

6. Be clear about your boundaries with those who offer advice. A simple "I appreciate your concern, but we're following a path that feels right for us" respects both your and the advisor's stance.

Practice Saying "No"

Like any skill, saying "No" becomes easier with practice. Start in low-stakes situations to build your confidence. Your "No" is just as important as your "Yes" in shaping the environment in which your child grows.

Balancing Act

When it comes to handling situations like the one with my dad at the wedding, it highlighted a crucial lesson in the dance of accepting and rejecting advice.

Empathy and Understanding

7. Recognize the place of love and concern advice often comes from, especially from family. Understanding their perspective can soften the interaction, even if the advice doesn't align with your approach.

Clear Communication

8. When boundaries are crossed, communicate your stance with love and clarity. It's not about confrontation but about affirming your role as the primary caregiver.

Seek Support

9. Sometimes, the weight of persistent advice feels too heavy. Lean on your husband, friends, or a support group who respects your parenting journey. They can offer the strength to stand firm in your decisions.

Challenges to Discovering Your "Yes" and Knowing Your "No"

One of my friends had been in the hospital for almost a week when one of her friends asked, "Since you're lying there all day anyway, would you have time to do some research and make a few phone calls for me?" And she still said, "Yes!"

Once you uncover your "Yes," you'd think it would be easier to identify your "No" and enforce it. But the line between the two can get hazy. There are a lot of reasons why we do not stick to our "No," such as guilt, appearances, and people-pleasing.

Guilt

You may feel guilty if your decision could hurt someone else's feelings. We need to be considerate of how our actions impact one another, but it goes both ways. People also need to consider how their expectations affect you. And just as you need to consider other people's feelings, they need to respect yours.

If your decision may hurt another person, it's wise to have a conversation with them so they will understand. Be open to their feedback. Their feelings are valid, and it's possible you may brainstorm a more mutually beneficial solution together. And, of course, pray on the issue and ask God what you should do. After you have prayerfully considered the other person's position, the decision is yours.

You have the right to say "No." Did you know that "No" is a complete sentence? This means there is nothing else you need to say. Don't feel like you need to apologize, make excuses, or over-explain. Very often, additional information only leads to rehashing a hard conversation.

Appearances

We've talked a lot about how we can fall into a comparison trap from spending too much time on social media. It's a powerful influence over our desire to keep up appearances. If you feel like you have to impress or compliment people to get their attention, then they are in the friendship for control or validation, not because they care about you. If people don't already like you for who you are, there's a good chance they're never going to like you.

If anyone asks you to do something that takes you away from your "Yes," then clearly, you need to say "No." I would urge you to just be you and let everybody else choose to either stay in your life or leave.

People Pleasing

Most relationships are never a perfectly equal give and take, but it's not worth maintaining contact with people who never give back. If you are constantly giving to people who are not there for you, then you need to say "No" to people pleasing. People who truly care about you will accept and respect your "No," even when it's not to their benefit.

I realize many people sincerely need help, and many of them are part of our bedrock, but you can't be everything to everyone. We need to recognize when we have become weary from over-extending ourselves.

I have said "Yes" to things that literally made my heart race, and I'd break out in a cold sweat. I would feel completely overwhelmed, and I still couldn't say "Yes" fast enough because I didn't want to upset people. I wanted to please people. In time, as I defined my "Yes," I also learned to say "No."

It's especially hard for Christian women to recognize and overcome people pleasing because the Bible tells us to give and help one another. But we have to please God before people, so your relationship with Him, His will, and His purpose for your life must come first. Even Jesus had limits to what He would give and when He would help.

There are several instances in the Bible where He said no to people who had selfish motives.

The only way to reinforce your boundaries is to be flexible when necessary, but know your "No." I hope this guides you through some of what you may have been wrestling with so you can discover the blessings inside your boundaries.

The Blessings Inside Your Boundaries

Do you remember my friend who did research while she lay in the hospital for a week? Years later, she decided enough was enough. She started saying "No" to people who showed their true motives. She also asked others to step in where needed so she could reclaim her life.

Then, my friend went back to work full time, got her college degree, and pursued her dreams. She discovered her purpose and the blessings of finding her "Yes" and knowing her "No."

Gain Control

When you are tied up in something you should have declined, you give up ownership of your time, efforts, and energy. You actually give up a part of your life.

I want you to think about that. When you don't say "No," you give up ownership and allow something else to control your life. That thing could take you away or shut down an opportunity to reach your goals and accomplish your "Yes." Guard your boundaries so people cannot take advantage of your time and energy.

Growth

One of the greatest gifts in reinforcing your boundaries is the growth and learning you gain through the experience. Don't let the lessons you have learned along the way and the things that you have experienced go to waste.

Strengthen Your Bedrock

When you learn to say "No," people show their real motives, and you find out who your friends are. It's better to have a few true friends than a million who are out for themselves. When you weed out the fluff, you are left with a strong bedrock of those who really care.

I have vetted my bedrock as I go through life with people. I allow them into my inner circle because I have had time to get to know them. I feel comfortable enough to let them into the rest of my life because they respect my boundaries.

Protecting Your Core

Boundaries protect your core so you can be authentic with yourself and others. Most people don't belong in your inner circle. They don't need to know your business, and it's not wise to leave yourself emotionally vulnerable and exposed. We all have things we don't want to speak of and experiences we don't want to share with others.

Our core is different for everyone. Some people are more fluid in the things they believe and how they want to live their lives. They leave things open to interpretation. That's okay, as long as it doesn't go against your core boundaries—the essence of who you are.

In order to protect your core, you have to know your "No" and be able to say that certain topics are off the table. Whatever those are, your "No" means you won't bend on them because they make up your character. For me, this includes my beliefs, my morals and ethics, and my faith. If advice or feedback hits against part of my core foundation and what I know to be true, it's an automatic "No." In preserving those boundaries, I have peace in walking out the path God has for me.

Be Ready for the "Yes"

If you get tied up in things you wish you had said "No" to, you cannot act on the next "Yes" that comes your way. Many times, the "No" you allowed blocks the very "Yes" you needed to make your next step forward.

I've declined wonderful opportunities because the timing wasn't right. God was preparing me for other priorities and getting me ready for the next season. If He intended for me to have the other opportunity, He will make it available when the time is right. But in order for me to step into that great next thing, I felt God really needed me to stay where I was until I felt that shift that would tell me, "The time is now."

Even if it's something you might enjoy, you need to ask if this is a good time. Consider if it would distract from more meaningful or important things.

No Limits

Why do we place limits on ourselves or allow others to place them on us? Is it because of fear, anxiety, shame, past experiences, or others' expectations? What have you allowed to limit your creativity, opportunity, growth, and dreams?

I want you to list the answers to these questions. This is your "No" list—the things you will begin to let go.

Saying "No" is not an act of giving up. It's claiming the freedom for your "Yes." Imagine what would be possible if you had no limits. Who can you become if you release all the limits that you or others have placed on you?

I am asking you to initiate and embrace change in your life. I know that's scary because it requires us to give up control, but when I try to control my life, I am held captive by stress. I have struggled to allow change and let go of control my whole life, but I'm learning that I'm not in control anyway. There's nothing to let go of because God has the master plan. He is in control of everything.

Please take this to heart: Let it go.

God has the plan to prosper you and not harm you. Ask yourself what role you play in the situation and what effect you can have. Can you change anything about the circumstances?

Write down your worries one by one. Assess if you really can make a difference in the things you are trying to control and if it's part of your "Yes." If so, move forward with prayer about the next steps. But if you realize you can't change the outcome, let it go.

By resisting change, you limit yourself and the blessings God has for you. Think about what is waiting to greet you on the other side when you live with no limits. The journey requires you to move and to let go of things you cannot control. But God is waiting on you to find your "Yes" and know your "No"—to live with no limits.

Grace in the Process

To discover your "Yes" is to know who you are. It was a long journey before I could say that I knew when to say "No" so I could be free to be steadfast with my "Yes." It's a beautiful way to live, and that's what I want for you. I challenge you to dig deep and embrace the journey to discover who you are. I want you to get to a place where you can be your "Yes" and know your "No."

Our life is built on saying "Yes" and "No," so do not let somebody else define who you are. I challenge you to claim the power God put inside you. If you do the work, if you seek your "Yes," evaluate your "Yes," and grow it, then you can become your "Yes."

When you start saying "No," you weed out things you don't need in your life, but you gain so much more than the absence of stress. There is peace and power in your "No." It may be uncomfortable at first, and it will take practice, but keep going. Claim your power by learning to say "No."

For a while, I lived with regret over all the time I wasted, especially when I thought of all the people I could have impacted if I had just said

"Yes" sooner. But God helped me understand that the time wasn't right earlier.

If you are struggling with regret, don't spend another moment in negativity. God's timing is always perfect, and He will make a way. He will open the doors and make sure the people who need your "Yes" will appear. Many of them will also be the people who help you in your journey.

Just get started and keep saying "Yes" every day.

It's an incredible and brave thing to go through the process of learning about yourself. I commend each of you on this journey, and I pray you will have discernment and the ability to hone in on who you really are and what you've been called to do. I pray you are willing to take the steps laid out before you that will help you fulfill the plan for your life.

I had no idea of the journey God was calling me to or where it would lead. I never could have imagined what He wanted me to do, who He would bring into my life, or what challenges I would face along the way.

I could not have dreamed of what He has done and how far He has taken me. I am so excited to see where the journey continues to go. Of course, I have not arrived at my final "Yes," and I hope I never do. It's a wonderful thing to get up every day and know you're going to discover something new about yourself or about the people around you.

Of course, life still has its challenges and hard seasons when anxiety and self-doubt lead me to wonder who I am. I try to put a mask over the insecurities that maybe I'm just not good enough or that I'm not worthy. God meets me in those times when I'm at my worst. He makes me vulnerable enough to be honest and face my fears so He can pull me out of self-doubt.

Even on good days, sometimes I still wear that mask. Without my relationship with God, I'd be completely lost. I've learned that when I neglect Him, I don't know the meaning of my life or how I even exist. That's why I lean on Him to get through each day one at a time. With His help, I can claim who I am authentically. I am comfortable being the wife, mother, and woman He created me to be.

Every day, I try to wrap that mask around who I am and know that it's okay to keep a little of it there. I think we all put on a little bit of a mask we won't fully take off. Not everybody deserves to have the full picture of who we really are. I don't have to share my full truth with everyone I meet. We can only be that vulnerable and truthful with people we trust. I think we need to keep the veil on that mask so we don't get hurt or taken advantage of by those who want to do just that.

Do you still recognize the person you see in the mirror? On days when the woman looking back at you is a stranger, please give yourself grace.

What do we mean by giving ourselves grace?

The word grace can also mean elegance or refined movement, but it's hard to be graceful when you're changing a dirty diaper.

To me, grace means allowing yourself a breath to say, "I know that something didn't go right, but it's going to be okay." It means allowing time to fix things, to change, and to grow from mistakes.

Giving yourself grace also means treating yourself with the same courtesy we give to others. You are understanding, accepting, and patient with other people when they mess up. Why would you not extend that same kindness to yourself?

In the Bible, grace is God's undeserved favor on our behalf. When Jesus paid the price for our sins, He saved us from the punishment we deserved. By dying for us, Jesus extended His love and acceptance to us. It's by His grace that we're saved.

So what does that have to do with unsolicited advice and knowing when to say "Yes" and when to say "No"?

Jesus died to give us the Father's grace, so who are we to deny it to ourselves?

Giving yourself grace means accepting yourself and being kind to yourself, just as God is to you. Jesus willingly gave us grace, so as we practice being kind to ourselves, we will be able to do it more freely.

We need to learn to value ourselves just as Jesus values us. That means accepting that even when we make mistakes, we still have value. Sometimes, it's hardest to forgive our own mistakes, but grace also means the ability to do through Jesus what we can't do on our own. As we lean on Him, we will grow in our ability to give grace to both ourselves and others.

Enforcing boundaries also involves giving yourself the grace to be who you really are. The more you learn through dealing with unsolicited advice and grow in setting boundaries, the more grace you give yourself. You have to give yourself the opportunity to be the mother that you are intended to be.

Unsolicited advice, social media, and other things we encounter are distractions and distortions. They are fluid, moving targets that try to define what it looks like to be a mother. In reality, we are most successful at being the best mothers we can be when we know ourselves, set our boundaries, enforce them, give ourselves grace, and allow ourselves to be the moms we always thought we were going to be.

Because of God's grace, we can be even better than we ever imagined.

REFLECTIONS

A Mother's Guide to Saying "No": Finding Strength in Scripture

In the tapestry of our lives as mothers, we are often pulled in myriad directions, tasked with nurturing, guiding, and protecting the tender souls entrusted to us. It's a role filled with joy, love, and, undoubtedly, challenges. Among these challenges is the art of saying "No"—not out of stubbornness, but from a place of wisdom, love, and, sometimes, necessary protection. Let's draw inspiration from Jesus, who, in His time on Earth, exemplified the strength of setting boundaries with grace and truth.

The Temptation of Christ (Matthew 4:1-11)

In the wilderness, Jesus was tempted by Satan, who offered Him all the kingdoms of the world in exchange for worship. Jesus said, "No," replying, "Away from me, Satan! For it is written: 'Worship the Lord your God, and serve him only'" (Matthew 4:10 NIV). Like Jesus, mothers are faced with daily temptations that veer us away from our true path. It may come in the form of societal pressures to conform to certain parenting styles or the allure of materialism overshadowing the values we wish to instill in our children. Saying "No" to these temptations means affirming our commitment to guiding our families with integrity and love.

The Wedding at Cana (John 2:1-11)

At the wedding at Cana, when the wine ran out, Jesus' mother, Mary, told Him about the situation, hinting at the need for His intervention.

Jesus responded, "Woman, why do you involve me?" (John 2:4 NIV), initially saying "No" to the request, indicating His time had not yet come. Yet, out of compassion and respect, He performed His first miracle, turning water into wine. This passage teaches us moms the delicate balance between saying "No" and being open to the needs of others. It's a reminder that our "No" is not always final but is discerned through prayer, compassion, and an understanding of God's timing.

Jesus Predicts His Death (Matthew 16:21-23)

When Jesus spoke of His upcoming suffering and death, Peter took Him aside and rebuked Him, saying, "'Never, Lord!' he said. 'This shall never happen to you!' Jesus turned and said to Peter, 'Get behind me, Satan! You are a stumbling block to me; you do not have in mind the concerns of God, but merely human concerns'" (Matthew 16:22-23 NIV).

In this stern "No," Jesus teaches us the importance of recognizing when well-intentioned advice or protection from loved ones may actually divert us from our God-given path. For mothers, this is a powerful reminder to discern the advice we receive, ensuring it aligns with God's will for us and our children, even when it means saying "No" to those we love.

Jesus' Purpose (Luke 4:42-43)

As Jesus' fame spread, the people of a town tried to keep Him from leaving. Jesus said, "No" to their desires, stating, "I must proclaim the good news of the kingdom of God to the other towns also, because that is why I was sent" (Luke 4:43 NIV). This illustrates the importance of saying "No" in order to fulfill our divine purpose. As mothers, our "No" can direct our focus and energy on our unique calling for our families, steering us toward actions that serve a greater purpose.

In embracing our "No," we align ourselves with a life that reflects not just our will but God's will for us and our children. Let these scriptural instances be a lantern on your path, guiding you in the sacred dance of setting boundaries with love, wisdom, and grace. Just as Jesus did, may you find the strength to say "No" with the assurance that in doing so, you are saying "Yes" to a higher calling, a deeper love, and a more profound commitment to the well-being of those you hold dear.

May this serve as a source of strength and encouragement, reminding you of the godly support that underpins every prayerful "No" spoken in love and wisdom.

Prayer

Heavenly Father,

Thank You for the gift of discernment, the wisdom to recognize when to say "Yes" and the courage to stand firm in our "No." In a world overflowing with voices, opinions, and persistent advice, help us to tune our hearts to Your voice above all else. Remind us that boundaries are not walls to keep others out but sacred spaces where Your peace and purpose flourish.

Lord, grant us the grace to navigate difficult conversations with humility and love, especially with those closest to us. Teach us to respond not out of frustration or fear, but with clarity, compassion, and respect. When we stumble, when we lose our temper, or when guilt creeps in, remind us that Your grace is more than enough to cover our mistakes. You meet us right where we are, offering forgiveness, growth, and the strength to try again.

Help us to find freedom in our "No" and purpose in our "Yes." Shape our hearts to reflect Your truth, our minds to align with Your wisdom, and our lives to honor the calling You've placed upon us as mothers, daughters, friends, and women of faith. May we walk confidently in the roles You've designed for us, trusting that we are exactly who our children, our families, and this world need—because You crafted us with intention.

Thank You, Lord, for being our constant guide, our ever-present help, and the source of unending grace. We lean into You, knowing that even when we feel overwhelmed, we are never alone. You are with us in every messy moment, every hard boundary, and every sacred yes.

In Jesus' name,

Amen.

Small Group Discussion Questions

1. Share a time when you had to assert boundaries with family or friends.
2. What are some core values or beliefs that guide your "Yes" in parenting? How do you stay true to these amidst varying opinions and advice?
3. Discuss the importance of saying "No" in certain situations. How can saying "No" be an act of love and protection for your family?
4. How do you balance enforcing boundaries with giving grace, both to yourself and to others who may overstep those boundaries?
5. Share an experience when you felt overwhelmed by emotions due to unsolicited advice or criticism. How did you manage your feelings and find a resolution?

Self-Care Affirmations

- I discern wisely between nurturing advice and what doesn't align with my path, trusting my inner voice.
- I am strong in setting healthy boundaries for my family's and my well-being.
- I respect my intuition and decisions in parenting, guided by love for my children.
- I give myself grace in moments of doubt, knowing I'm doing my best with what I have.
- My value as a mother is defined by my love and commitment, not by others' opinions.
- In the face of uninvited opinions, I maintain peace, knowing I am the keeper of my family's happiness.
- I embrace the joys and challenges of parenting with a resilient and loving heart.

CHAPTER SEVEN
SEEKING ADVICE

Disclaimer:

This chapter touches on the deeply sensitive subject of the loss of a child. While it aims to provide comfort and understanding, readers who may find this topic particularly distressing are advised to approach with care.

When you need to make a decision or solve a problem, whose input do you ask for first? Your own, right? Typically, I'll have several conversations with me, myself, and I, and sadly, none of us knows the answer. Sometimes, I say to myself, "You're crazy today, girl. Take your medication, and then maybe we'll talk."

One of these days, I'll figure out to start with prayer first. Kudos to you if you're already there. But if the internal trio of me, myself, and I are too embroiled in a debate to catch on to the whisper of divine guidance, it's perhaps time to seek wisdom from those God places in our path. That's precisely what I did during a harrowing chapter of life, haunted by the fear of losing one of my precious boys.

My husband Luke and I were well into our parenting journey with two young boys under the age of six. Something inside me had felt amiss and unsettled for a while, but I couldn't identify why. A gnawing sense of unease had taken root in my soul, a puzzle I couldn't piece together, so I prayed for God to help me understand and soothe my heart's unrest.

During one of our weekly evening adult Bible study sessions, an ordinarily quiet woman shared a story relating to our discussion and wrapped it by saying, "And that's when I lost my son." Her words struck a chord so deep within me that it was as if a veil had been lifted, exposing my deepest fear—I, too, was going to face the loss of a child. Panic seized me. Was it one of my boys? Or a child yet unknown?

After she finished her story, the woman bowed her head as the group leader commended her courage in sharing and her strength to lean on God through such a devastating loss. All I could do was sit there while tears stained her Bible. The silence that followed her story was heavy; her bravery in sharing such a profound loss was acknowledged with reverence. But there I sat, immobilized by grief for a future I prayed would never come to pass. The very idea of enduring faith through the loss of a child was something I couldn't bear.

Sometimes, a glimpse of something to come brings comfort to pull you through. But this was no comfort! I was full of questions and fear! We almost lost Cameron during his birth, and I absolutely knew I could not endure losing either of my boys. The last thing I wanted to be known for was my faith through the journey of losing a child!

My mind raced with endless what-ifs, leaving me paralyzed. I couldn't share these fears with my husband without seeming lost in my imagination. Yet, after nights of turmoil and fervent prayers, I finally sought solace from my pastor's wife, a beacon of wisdom and comfort. When I shared my story, she didn't frown upon me, judge me, or tell me to dismiss seemingly unfounded fears. She listened, paused before replying, and said, "I feel like God is giving me a verse for you. It's 2 Timothy 1:7, 'For God has not given us a spirit of fear, but of power and of love and of a sound mind'" (NKJV).

I clung to this verse, and it became a stronghold for me—a daily declaration over my family.

Months went by as I continued to lean on God for peace, and in time, a friend's visit unveiled the heartbreaking clarity of my apprehensions. As we caught up on what had happened in our lives, she shared that she had a miscarriage prior to the birth of her first son.

Just like at the Bible study, her words washed over my heart as the answer to many months of prayer made itself painfully known: We would lose a child through miscarriage. It was a bittersweet confirmation that neither of our two living sons would be taken.

Knowing When to Get Help

Sometimes, we pray for a peek into the future and get it. Just like absorbing an unexpected shock, knowing in advance is still traumatic. However, there was hope in the message as I continued to pray my story would be different.

We became pregnant a few months later. I loved each moment of being pregnant with our baby. I sang songs to my child and patted my tummy, all while still praying for faith and guidance. The foreknowledge of our loss did little to cushion the blow when it came. We lost our third child a few months into the pregnancy. No amount of mental preparation can brace one for the all-consuming grief of loss, of saying goodbye to a soul you never got to hold yet loved so deeply.

I am so grateful for the peace my pastor's wife delivered through acceptance and discernment. And I'll never be able to truly articulate the hope in the confirmation through my friend's bravery in sharing her story. The confirmation of things to come did not make it easier, but God used two loving women to build my faith through the trial.

I have learned that the process of seeking advice, accepting confirmation of the answer, and moving forward in implementation can be very difficult. The answers to my unrest came from unlikely sources, but their wisdom was confirmed by God. I thought walking it out would be easier, but I was mistaken. Many times, I felt driven to darkness—to places where I did not feel God's presence in my life, even though I knew He was always there.

That's why recognizing the need for help is such a gift. It takes incredible strength and vulnerability to reach out. Celebrate that gift.

Imagine you're in a game of dodgeball, and you get hit so hard that you fall, and you notice a bone sticking out of your leg. Immediately, you think, "My leg is broken."

What will you do? You'll go to the hospital, right? You would never try to just pretend it's not there and that everything is fine.

And when you get to the hospital, what will you tell the doctors? You'd scream, "Please fix my broken leg!" You certainly wouldn't sit there quietly until someone in a white coat asks how you're doing and then respond with, "Well, Doc, I'm not too sure. This here leg doesn't feel right. Do you think it's broken?"

Sometimes, the damage isn't as obvious, but it is no less real or painful. You may feel unsettled, like something is amiss, but you can't articulate why.

It's hard to pinpoint, but you just don't really feel like you're in the game. We all feel pain, both seen and unseen. Life throws dodgeballs, curveballs, and fastballs, and they're gonna leave a mark. It's okay to acknowledge that it doesn't feel right. But just like with physical issues, the only way to get the help you need for emotional or mental suffering is to see a doctor.

God designed us to seek advice, so acknowledging the symptoms is the only way to make it right. We ask others what they think because we are hardwired for connection. Sure, you could go and live as a hermit forever, but your growth and your life would be stagnant. While some people may be able to live better in isolation, the majority of us need one another to thrive.

Building Your Support Team

We are hardwired for connection because, without it, most of us can't survive. For example, studies have shown that if a baby is fed and changed but lacks the stimulation of human interaction, its development will be affected. Healthy babies whose physical needs are met but are otherwise neglected sometimes die.

It's the same through all stages of life. When we feel isolated and alone, our natural desire for connection intensifies. We all need that sense of connection in order to thrive. Reaching out for help is completely normal and necessary. When you feel isolated and alone, it's because you're lacking the connection you need to thrive.

While our support group helps us navigate through difficult times, it's important to recognize when and how to actively seek out connections beyond our immediate circle. The first step is often the hardest, but it's something we all must do. No one can read your mind, so it's up to you to reach out and ask for help. Just remember that you're not alone.

Many women hesitate to ask for help because they don't want to be a burden or cause worry. In chapter five, we talked about Galatians 6:2, which says, "Bear one another's burdens, and so fulfill the law of Christ." I think many of us misunderstand this verse to believe that we are a burden, as in some kind of oppression or intrusion.

A *burden* is a self-serving, one-sided friendship. Instead of feeling bothered by a genuine friend in need, I struggle to know they suffered and endured alone rather than reaching out.

We also need to remember that an overwhelming weight for you is not as heavy as it is for someone who loves you. In fact, both of you will feel lighter when they offer prayer, comfort, and wise counsel.

God expects us to walk on both sides of Scripture. People can't share your burden if they don't know you need help. When you reach out, you are giving your loved one the opportunity to be used by God and fulfill the law of Christ by showing you love and support.

A refusal to ask for advice can be a surrender to toxic situations. If you are in a place where you don't feel safe to be yourself, know that you don't have to tolerate mistreatment. Your voice and your feelings are valid. God cares about you, and He wants you to seek out those with whom you feel comfortable.

It's important to be selective about the connections we make. Our relationship with God is our key source of peace, so we need to filter the advice through our values and the Word of God. It's important to build your team of reliable sources of advice and support, whether it's a loved one, a counselor, or a trusted person in your community.

Do you remember the honor and empowerment of being the dodgeball team captain? Me neither, but I always imagined how amazing it would be to assemble the perfect team. I'd pick the fastest, strongest kids.

I'd pick the ones who knew when to duck, when to jump, and when to warn me if an opponent was taking aim. We'd be so awesome that every opposing team would be eliminated before they could throw a single ball.

You may have missed the opportunity to assemble your dream team in elementary school, but you can do it as a mom. Your bedrock is your team. They are the ones you trust to look out for you. Your bedrock consists of the people who will reinforce the hedges around your family to keep the good in and the bad out. They are quick to recognize irrelevant advice, and they have sound decision-making skills.

In dodgeball, the goal is to be the last kid standing, but in parenting, your strongest teammates are blocking and dispersing hazards on their knees. They are your prayer warriors. They know you well enough, and they have the discernment to give you the faith nuggets you'll cling to.

The people from whom you seek advice aren't perfect, but they know how to play the game of life. They have lived enough to learn and grow from their experiences. They are stable; they are people you look up to and respect. Just like you, their heart is in the right place, and they are trying to live out their faith and their purpose.

It's crucial to confide in someone who won't judge you or spread your business to the entire world. Those you allow in your bedrock accept you for who you are, and they understand the importance of privacy and discretion.

I had complete trust in the pastor's wife because I witnessed her navigate through life with grace and wisdom, serving as a mentor to many. I never heard her share other people's stories, and I never felt judged. She always made me feel heard and understood. I also knew that she always prayed before speaking.

You want to be selective in who you share your innermost heart and thoughts with, especially as it involves something as cherished as your children. Not everyone deserves access to your full truth.

Asking for Advice

It is crucial to be discerning about the advice you receive, both unsolicited and solicited. Just like you must evaluate the motive and the source when people offer unsolicited advice, you want to ask yourself the same questions before asking for advice. Take a moment to reflect on whether the person's heart is aligned with the things you value and believe in.

Let's start with strangers. You may ask for input from individuals who appear to have similar experiences or lifestyles. For example, you can form a quick, vague opinion of a woman with kids and a stroller, a bulging diaper bag, and messy hair. It's likely she's living through some of the same crazy you are. But if she also looks a little shell-shocked, ask her to blink twice to tell you if she's safe before you ask for her input. If she doesn't seem to respond, I'd recommend praying for her instead of asking how she manages to balance work and family life.

While advice from a stranger comes totally void of context, there is a possible upside. She may be more honest because she doesn't know you well enough to care if you take offense.

Asking for advice from friends can be tricky. A good friend has your back no matter what, but they also may sugar-coat the advice for fear of hurting your feelings. But your best friends (or perhaps those loving sisters) will be honest to the point you want to smack their face a little bit.

Those are the women you want to lead your team, the ones who love you enough to tell you what you need to hear, whether you like it or not. The subtle bus left the station ten years ago, and they shoot straight for the mic-drop, which is exactly why we seek their advice first. Sometimes, we hate those precious, invaluable friends almost as much as we love them, especially when they are right.

Now, let's talk about family. Some family members may have ulterior motives or be concerned about upsetting you and losing out on their inheritance. They really want grandma's ring, so they'll tell you what they think you want to hear. It's important to be aware of these dynamics when seeking their advice. You want to make sure that the person you turn to for advice shares your heart alignment so you can confidently accept and implement their guidance in your life.

No matter who you ask, always evaluate the advice you receive and discard what doesn't resonate with you. Instead of carrying the burdens of other people's opinions, take the time to evaluate where you are, seek help when needed, and choose what you will carry for the long haul.

My momma always told me to be careful who you ask to pray for you because they just might pray against you. Surround yourself with prayer partners who are truly on your team and aligned with your values.

Seeking advice can be beneficial, but it's essential to be discerning about the source and motive of the advice. Choose wisely, trust your intuition, and remember that, ultimately, you are the one who knows what's best for your life.

Considering Feedback

Kelsey knew from experience that Sunday School and kid's Christmas programs were not her thing, so she was excited to serve a more mature audience in her new church. Her true passion was missionary work, so she joined the adult missionary program to mentor men and women interested in proclaiming the gospel in some of the most unreached corners of the world.

However, when she began her role as the Missions Coordinator, she found that most participants came in with rose-colored expectations, naïve to the openly hostile sentiment toward Christianity in certain parts of the world. When Kelsey explained the risks of preaching the gospel in such remote areas and how to handle threatening situations, most people never returned to class.

Kelsey made an appointment with her pastor to brainstorm ways to better prepare adults for missionary work. During the meeting, she explained the problem and asked for advice about how to improve either the course curriculum or her delivery so more people would stay to learn the skills and discernment needed for missionary work before deciding they couldn't do it. The pastor agreed to consult with church elders, pray on it, and get back to her.

A few weeks later, the pastor gave her unexpected news. The elder committee thought she was the perfect candidate to fill what they knew was a long-standing need in the church. The pastor asked Kelsey to write a curriculum to introduce missionary work to teenagers. After the curriculum was written, she would then teach the Sunday School staff and the first few courses to test the program and get it off the ground.

Kelsey was stunned. The last thing she wanted was to go back to working with youth. It just wasn't her gifting. When she reminded the pastor that what she needed was to improve the existing curriculum, he replied, "Kelsey, you came to me asking how to better prepare adults for missionary work. I want you to pray on it and ask if this is where God wants you to show up. If so, then it's not up to you to resist Him. You said the adults were naïve and unprepared. So, prepare them. This is your chance to educate the next generation of adults you will work with as Missions Coordinator."

The truth is, the details of "Kelsey's" story have been altered to protect both the guilty and the innocent, but I learned several things during my role in a similar experience. First, you can't ask for advice but then put parameters around it. Kelsey asked the pastor how to improve either the curriculum or her delivery. While her willingness to learn and grow as an instructor is commendable, she wasn't willing to hear about other alternatives.

Has anyone ever asked you for advice only to immediately shoot it down? I bet your response was something like, "Why did you ask for my opinion if you weren't willing to listen for even a moment? Don't come to me next time!"

When we intentionally seek out help, we can't apply conditions and attach strings to which types of advice we will take into consideration, which leads me to the next lesson.

If you're going to seek advice, you'd better be willing to take it into consideration. Everything that happens in your life is important to you. It's the same for anybody else. The things they have walked through, even if they don't seem like a big deal to you, are a very big deal to them. They've spent time thinking about it and wondering, "Did I do this right? Could I have done better? Where was the growth? What lesson did I learn?"

You've already vetted who you will ask. You've determined this person's experience has value for your situation and that you trust them. When you ask for advice, you've asked that person to share their mistakes, challenges, and lessons. You've asked them to be vulnerable and perhaps share details about their loved ones.

If someone willingly offers you a piece of their heart, don't dismiss them. You came to them for a different perspective, so embrace their feedback. Consider the life experience that person went through to gain the wisdom they've shared.

Considering their feedback does not assume immediate, off-the-shelf implementation. It means you'll listen and think about what they have to offer. It's possible the advice can be adapted to your situation. Perhaps God intended the wisdom for your future self or for someone else you'll meet later.

A lot of unsolicited advice doesn't deserve a single brain cell of our energy, but I never discount the advice I request. Don't take their gift and their vulnerability for granted because you never know when or for whom the advice may be helpful.

Last, as you consider the advice, be willing to accept it even if it's hard. Many times, the best advice is the hardest to implement and walk through. We talked about the people who love you enough to tell it like it is whether you like it or not. That is an especially vulnerable and risky move that requires self-sacrificial love. She knows you may be upset, but her heart is to help you grow. A friend who skips telling you what you want to hear to tell you what she truly believes you need to hear is putting your needs above her own.

Confirmation

Whether the advice is what you want to hear or not, the most important thing is to consult God for confirmation at every step. God's confirmation is key to determining if, when, or how to implement the advice.

Confirmation can come from anywhere. According to a popular pastor, David Hernandez, there are three signs that God is confirming you are walking in His will.[4] All three signs were manifest when I had my first miscarriage.

The first is that there will be clarity on how to apply Scripture to your circumstances. God will reveal a Bible verse and how to walk it out in this season. When I confided in my pastor's wife, she prayed before speaking and then told me she felt like God was giving me a specific verse, 2 Timothy 1:7. In the days that followed, I pondered the verse, and God showed me how to apply it not only to my current situation but to my whole life.

The second sign that God is confirming a decision is that multiple events will fall into place to allow the situation to move forward. Many times, we observe this through what appears to be a series of coincidences where things just seem to line up like dominos. The necessary doors open, and God provides the resources to accomplish His will.

The woman at the Bible study was the first confirmation for me. My pastor's wife was the second, and my friend was the third. They came one after another, and it all lined up.

Third, there will be peace and contentment in your heart even as you walk through hard times. Philippians 4:7 says, "And the peace of God, which surpasses all understanding, will guard your hearts and your minds through Christ Jesus."

We have to find a place of peace in the chaos to let things unfold when life is hard. When circumstances are completely beyond our control, we have to wait and continue to pray and cling to our faith so we can relax in the peace of knowing we are doing the best we can.

When I implement advice without that peace, I find myself running fast, hard, and long. I'm antsy and unsettled. When I have received other confirmation, and I'm at peace with it, I can act on it and then let it go. God's peace is solid, and it never changes. Events around me will still upset me, but I still rest in His peace with my choices.

Biblical guidance, open doors, and inexplicable peace are all signs that God is confirming a decision. Even when these signs exist, sometimes we question if we are really hearing from God. We wonder if we are just seeing what we want to see, or we might want to make sure of what He is really asking us to do.

Applying this list to our decision-making increases our certainty in God's confirmation and will for our lives. For example, you can verify the confirmation is, in fact, from God if you experience biblical guidance, open doors, and inexplicable peace simultaneously and in alignment. You also may receive biblical confirmation that your understanding and application of Scripture is sound.

God uses other people to confirm His will for us, and His confirmation is not a one-and-done. This means you must seek advice to discover how to follow His lead. Then, His repeated confirmations continue to tell you, "This is My path for you." It all begins with making sure you have the right filters and the right people in your life.

The confirmation should be directly in line with emotions that fill you with peace. If your final answer isn't accompanied by peace, then there will be resistance as you implement it with your family.

If the solution isn't accompanied by peace in your heart, you're going to struggle to implement it within your family. That's why knowing yourself and your boundaries and holding firmly to them is so important.

Seeking advice and God's confirmation ties in with becoming your "Yes" and knowing your "No." If you have gone through the process to know who you want to be as a parent and a family, then if outsiders disagree, it's their problem, not yours. They are not in your shoes going forward in the sacred job of parenting. They do not know your child like you do, and they do not see what God has revealed to you.

When you have the right team of your best friends, mentors, professionals, and family members, and you've allowed God to lead, then there should be peace in the implementation, even amid resistance.

And there *will* be resistance.

Implementing Change

They say the only one who likes change is a soiled baby, but we know that's not true either. In the beginning, the kids may be the biggest source of resistance. Have you ever met a three-year-old who says, "Yeah, Mommy, I like it that you don't give me a snack in the afternoon anymore. And I can't wait for the moment you lay me down for bed and immediately walk out the door. I never cared for forty-five minutes of stories, snuggles, and songs anyway."

You're most vulnerable when you're implementing changes because that's when you become a target. As you work to put new things into practice, you will meet pushback from people who don't agree with your decision. Family members or friends who don't have the same beliefs may not like your new boundaries. Many people don't want you to have what they long for. But if you have gone through the process to make a decision confirmed by God and wrapped in peace, why would you let anybody who's not even on your team break through your barriers?

You have to have some secure, strong boundaries in place to overcome that resistance. Having peace about what you're implementing is key. Peace will help you guard your boundaries and go ahead with your plan, disregarding the resistance. As you implement the advice, extend grace to yourself, the person who gave you the advice, and to those adjusting to the changes. Remember the tears, prayers, and sleepless nights that brought you here. Remember how vulnerable and brave you had to be in seeking advice.

There's always going to be resistance, but it will be easier for you to implement your solution if you have already put it through your process. If you've taken the right steps and you have peace about it, you can be sure that, in the long run, it's going to create more peace in your family.

One of the proudest moments of my motherhood journey was when Austin was five. Not only did my little boy show me how smart he was, but he did it right in front of Grandpa. It was one of the hottest days of the summer when Austin came into the house from playing outside. He shut the door, wiped the sweat off his forehead, and declared, "Momma, it's hot as hell outside!" I busted out laughing and said, "Yes, it is, Baby, it certainly is!"

Dad just looked at me slack-jawed and wide-eyed until Austin skipped upstairs. Then he said, "Andrea, were you actually listening to the mouth on that boy? Aren't you going to discipline him?"

I laughed, "No, Daddy. At age five, he already knows heaven and hell are real. He knows that hell is a real place of suffering, that it's hot, and he doesn't want to go there. Isn't that the number one thing you want your kids to know? And not only that, but he used the word in proper context. That's my boy!"

Y'all, I was thrilled with my little man that day. I thought it was the best thing he had ever done in his young life. My heart was beaming, "Well done, Baby!" I wasn't disciplining him, and I wasn't sorry!

Momma, God made your tiny human so that only you can care for them! You have the power to know who God made you to be inside of you. You are unique, loved, and required! Understand who you are and what works for you!

Every parent's experience is different because every kid is different. Everyone responds differently, even when dealing with similar situations because you interpret them differently based on your life experiences. Even identical twins have unique responses to the same environmental circumstances. Everything is up for interpretation, so you need to make decisions for your family based on your beliefs, your character, your faith, and your knowledge of each child.

At the end of the day, we are each just trying to raise our babies, lighten our loads, survive, and thrive through this journey of motherhood! You've got this! I know this because you are engaged with other moms, seeking, encouraging, and building a stronger community to journey through motherhood together.

Proverbs 4:23 says, "Keep your heart with all diligence, For out of it spring the issues of life." Your heart is a sacred place. You can't let any old thing get in there! God wants you to process, filter, and glean from others to make the best decisions for you and your family.

Others mean well, but there will be times you will have to stand your ground. Have the courage to empty the diaper bag and take stock of what's inside to determine what to keep and what to throw away.

If things don't work out the way we hoped for, we still know we've done what we needed to. We've gone through our process of seeking wise counsel and confirmation through prayer. So many times, we try to get in there and fix things. But we only muddle things up and get in God's way when we stick our fingers in it. If God has brought you to a place of peace, then know you've done everything you can. Now rest, wait, and let life unfold.

Be the Best Version of Yourself

Grace is a pertinent part of your story and your journey. If it isn't, then it should be. You need to allow yourself to be yourself and to be flexible enough to know that no parent in the history of this world has ever done it all right.

Trust yourself. You may choose to parent just like those around you expect, or you may choose to parent outside the social norms. But whatever you do, don't let doubt sneak in to take hold, cause stress, and attack your self-worth as a mom! Don't dim your light by comparing yourself to someone else's journey! Be you.

I love the life verse God gave me because 2 Timothy 1:7 gives me comfort; it reminds me to lean on God, and it makes me laugh. It says that God gave us a sound mind, but some days, I wonder! I feel like I'm searching for that sound mind, and for the life of me, I can't remember where I left her!

Then, I see her. I get a glimpse of the woman God created me to be. Indeed, she has power and a sound mind, and my goodness—that woman is bold. Someday, when I truly embrace and step into that sound mind, it's going to be awesome.

Mommas, that verse is for you too. God has given you the spirit to boldly walk into your sound mind, the best version of yourself. He gave you power and courage to be your authentic true self and to use your gifts and purpose to serve and glorify Him. Own it, girl.

I have had conversations with women where we share how we feel like we're gradually losing pieces of ourselves until we don't know who we are anymore. Some of that is meant to be. It happens naturally because you're giving it away in love. Those are the good things to give away.

But sometimes, it feels like those pieces are taken from us, like we lost them against our will. Perhaps you didn't even realize it until you felt a sense of loss and looked back to see a piece of your heart in someone else's fist. If that's you today, please know you are loved, you are not alone, and it's not too late.

The reason you feel worthless is because you have let other people devalue the worth of your "Yes." To say "Yes" to yourself, you must stand and say, "No, not anymore—I'm not listening to you. I appreciate your input, but today is a *no* for you. I don't have to take what you are dishing out today. I'm going to make my own recipe."

Don't give away pieces of your core because if you do, people will rewire who you are. God did not give any human being the right, the power, or the permission to define your purpose. How dare someone else say you are not worthy! When did God surrender His authority to write your story? Who among us has the right to question God's masterpiece?

Dear sister, if you are reading this now or if you wake up one day and feel that your voice has been taken from you, know you have the power to take it back one "Yes" and one "No" at a time. And it's normal to grieve the pieces of yourself and the time you've lost, but God will use every moment of your life for good if you let Him.

In the darkness and stillness, He was using every single one of these challenges in your life to help you become the person you are today. There is no other way for you to get to where you're going than to continue from where you've been.

God is busy making a uniquely qualified mom in you so you can impact your children in the way He needs you to. You are more precious for having been through the fire, and now you can watch the blessings unfold as you walk toward Him. They may not come in the timing or in the way you hoped or can understand, but just keep saying "Yes" to yourself and keep saying "Yes" to Him. Keep saying, "Yes, I am worthy because God says so." And nobody can take that worth away from you.

REFLECTIONS

Hannah's Faith and Trust in God

Scripture Reading: 1 Samuel 1:9-11, 26-28, and 2:1-2

Hannah's story is a powerful testament to faith, perseverance, and the ultimate act of trust in God. As we reflect on her journey, we can draw parallels to our own lives, especially when faced with the profound challenges of parenting and the fear of losing a child. Let's delve into Hannah's story and uncover the lessons it holds for us today.

Hannah longed for a child but faced years of barrenness. In her deep anguish, she turned to God in prayer. "She was deeply distressed and prayed to the LORD and wept bitterly. And she vowed a vow and said, 'O LORD of hosts, if you will indeed look on the affliction of your servant and remember me and not forget your servant, but will give to your servant a son, then I will give him to the LORD all the days of his life, and no razor shall touch his head'" (1 Samuel 1:10-11).

God answered Hannah's heartfelt prayer, and she bore a son, Samuel. True to her vow, Hannah dedicated Samuel to the Lord. She said, "As soon as the child is weaned, I will bring him, so that he may appear in the presence of the LORD and dwell there forever" (1 Samuel 1:22). When the time came, she brought Samuel to Eli, the priest, and said, "Oh, my lord! As you live, my lord, I am the woman who was standing here in your presence, praying to the LORD. For this child I prayed, and the LORD has granted me my petition that I made to him. Therefore I have lent him to the LORD. As long as he lives, he is lent to the LORD" (1 Samuel 1:26-28).

Despite the heartache of giving her son to the Lord's service, Hannah praised God for His faithfulness. She declared, "My heart exults in the

LORD; my horn is exalted in the LORD. My mouth derides my enemies, because I rejoice in your salvation. There is none holy like the LORD: for there is none besides you; there is no rock like our God" (1 Samuel 2:1-2).

Lessons for Moms

Hannah's story teaches us several profound lessons about faith, trust, and the surrender of our deepest fears to God.

Turning to God in Distress: When faced with overwhelming fears and challenges, like the anxiety of losing a child, we must turn to God first. Hannah's immediate reaction was to pour her heart out to the Lord. "Humble yourselves, therefore, under the mighty hand of God so that at the proper time he may exalt you, casting all your anxieties on him, because he cares for you" (1 Peter 5:6-7).

Trusting God's Plan: Hannah's vow and her subsequent actions demonstrate her unwavering trust in God's plan, even when it meant personal sacrifice. Trusting God requires faith that His ways are higher than ours. "Trust in the LORD with all your heart, and do not lean on your own understanding. In all your ways acknowledge him, and he will make straight your paths" (Proverbs 3:5-6).

Surrendering Our Fears: Hannah's surrender of Samuel to God's service is a powerful example of giving our fears and our children over to God. As parents, we must learn to release control and trust that God will care for our children. "For God gave us a spirit not of fear but of power and love and self-control" (2 Timothy 1:7).

Praising God in All Circumstances: Despite the heartache, Hannah praised God, recognizing His goodness and faithfulness. This teaches us to maintain a heart of gratitude and worship, even in difficult times. "Rejoice in the Lord always; again I will say, rejoice" (Philippians 4:4).

Application

Hannah's story shows us the necessity of seeking God's guidance and leaning on Him for peace. My own fear about facing the potential loss of a child and finding comfort through prayer and wise counsel echoes Hannah's experience. It reminds us to cling to God's promises and to trust in His perfect plan, even when it is hard to understand.

Practical Steps:

1. **Pray and Surrender:** When faced with fears or challenges, start with prayer. Surrender your anxieties to God, trusting that He is in control.
2. **Seek Godly Counsel:** Surround yourself with wise, godly people who can offer support and advice. Listen to their counsel and seek God's confirmation through Scripture and prayer.
3. **Maintain a Heart of Praise:** Cultivate an attitude of gratitude. Praise God for His faithfulness and trust in His plan, even in the midst of trials.
4. **Trust God with Your Children:** Release your children into God's care, believing that He loves them even more than you do and will guide their lives according to His perfect will.

Hannah's story is a testament to the power of faith, prayer, and surrender. As we navigate the challenges of parenting and face our deepest fears, let us follow Hannah's example by turning to God, trusting His plan, and praising Him through it all.

Prayer

Dear Heavenly Father, thank You for the example of Hannah's faith and trust in You. Help us to surrender our fears and anxieties to You, especially when it comes to our children. Grant us the wisdom to seek Your guidance and the peace that comes from trusting in Your perfect plan. May we always praise You, knowing that You are our rock and our salvation.

In Jesus' name,

Amen.

Small Group Discussion Questions

1. Reflect on a time when you faced a significant challenge. Did you turn to God first? Why or why not?
2. How can we develop a habit of seeking God's guidance in times of distress?
3. Share an experience when trusting in God's plan led to a positive outcome, even if it wasn't what you expected.
4. How do you handle fear and anxiety? What helps you surrender these emotions to God?
5. How can we cultivate a heart of praise and gratitude during difficult times?
6. How has godly counsel impacted your decisions? How can we build a network of trusted advisors?

7. What are some areas in your life where you need to release control and trust God more?

8. How have trials strengthened your faith and trust in God? What role does your community play in this process?

Self-Care Affirmations

- I am deserving of peace and will seek God first for comfort.
- I trust God's plan and believe He will give me strength.
- I release my fears to God, embracing His power and love.
- I seek godly counsel and value the support of others.
- I choose gratitude and praise in all circumstances.
- I am a unique, valuable mother, equipped by God for this journey.

CHAPTER EIGHT

LEARNING IS A PROCESS AND MISTAKES ARE INEVITABLE

Every family game night brings its own excitement, especially when the Old Maid deck comes out. It's a game that's simple yet filled with suspense as each player draws a card, hoping not to be the one left holding the Old Maid. The tension rises with each turn, and the relief when you pass off that dreaded card is palpable, followed by a groan from someone else at the table when they end up stuck with it. The person who deals or passes on the Old Maid card is like a dirty diaper dealer. They can stink up your whole game in no time!

In this game of life, where advice and opinions are often dealt as freely as cards in Old Maid, we'll explore how to gracefully work with the hands we're dealt. Whether we're dealing the cards, dodging the Old Maid, or navigating through the unsolicited advice we receive, there's always a way to reshuffle for a better outcome.

Becca's Story

Can giving suggestions or asking questions about another mom's situation with her kids be taken the wrong way? Have you ever been told to back off? If so, how did you receive that feedback, and what action did you take? Are you still friends today?

Lean in for my friend Becca's story about the incredible gift of friendship that overcame the hurt of unsolicited parenting advice.

One day, Becca's friend Sarah shared a private matter about her son's mysterious, ongoing illness. After several years of debilitating symptoms, the doctors were unable to diagnose the issue. Sarah was a private woman, so Becca was both surprised with the news and grateful for Sarah's trust and confidence in her.

Becca and Sarah had been friends for years, and Becca cared deeply for Sarah's family, so, of course, she wanted to help. Becca prayed for the family and researched all she could in hopes of finding helpful information for the doctors. Over the next six months, Becca checked in with Sarah weekly to report her findings, get progress updates on recent medical tests, and offer help.

While Becca's response came from love, she missed the signs that her messages were leaving Sarah increasingly doubtful of her ability to care for her family.

Sarah was already under the crippling weight of caring for a chronically sick child, and Becca's uninvited interrogation wasn't helping. It's not like Sarah wasn't trying to advocate for her son. Couldn't Becca see that Sarah was already doing everything she could?

As she watched her son's childhood unfold in suffering, Sarah agonized over her own inability to find answers and relief for her little one. Why couldn't she just make it all disappear? Why couldn't she protect her son so he could enjoy childhood like the other boys? Did other moms think she was inadequate too? Worse yet, does her own son think Sarah wasn't pushing the doctors hard enough?

While she couldn't take the pain away, Sarah did her best to comfort and encourage her son, all while desperately wishing for a friend who would do the same for her own broken momma's heart.

Sarah needed a friend to believe in her and not doubt her every move. She needed a friend to support her, not fix her. All these years, she thought Becca was that friend. One day, Sarah just couldn't take it anymore. She picked up the phone, prayed, "Lord, please help me," and called Becca.

Becca answered, "Hey, friend! I'm glad you called! I've been thinking of you and praying for you. I wanted to tell you what I found online. Have your doctors tested for this disease my niece has? Give me a minute; I'll look up the name of it again."

Sarah spoke up, "Becca, please stop. We need to talk. Our friendship will suffer if certain things don't change."

In an instant, Becca's world held still. She listened to the feedback, expressed her intent to help, and apologized for the hurt. Sarah graciously accepted the apology, but as soon as the call ended, Becca burst into tears.

In shock and disbelief, she stepped back to consider what she may have done to cause Sarah to feel criticized. Many of the conversations were through text, so Becca scrolled through her messages, searching for anything that could have been interpreted critically. Maybe she was too forward. Perhaps she could have softened her approach. Did she ignore Sarah's hurt responses to the advice?

As Becca scrolled through the messages, she remembered a game she played with her daughter. Ever since the girl got her license, she had turned into the family's expert backseat driver. Rather than leave her at the next intersection, Becca made a game of it called "You said; I heard." For example, if the daughter said, "You missed the turn for the fastest route," then Becca would reply, "Okay, you said, 'You missed the best turn, but I heard, 'You don't know where you are going, and I'm not going to make it home in time for next year!'"

Becca also remembered her own agonizing journey through caring for a chronically sick child and how easy it is to perceive things in a way other than what is intended. As she read concerned messages like "Why aren't the doctors pushing hard enough?" and "Maybe they don't believe your child because he's so young," Becca realized that what Sarah heard was, "Why aren't you advocating for your child?" or "Maybe he's not really that sick."

Just as revealing as what Becca found is what she didn't find—a request or permission from Sarah for help. Sarah never even hinted that she welcomed Becca's opinion. Instead, Becca wedged herself into Sarah's family matters.

Becca was stunned that she hadn't recognized what she was doing until Sarah spoke up. As Becca wept over how she had hurt her dear friend, she realized her own intent behind the advice was irrelevant. The only thing that mattered was how Sarah perceived the feedback. Despite Becca's intentions, all the advice accomplished was to add fuel to the fire raging inside her friend's heart. When Becca went into fix-it mode, Sarah felt broken.

Becca contacted Sarah to tell her that she realized her behavior was intrusive and critical. She took full responsibility for her mistakes and apologized again. Sarah accepted Becca's apology and assured her that the friendship was good, so they could leave it in the past. Going forward, Becca knew that certain topics were guarded for Sarah. Some parts of her life were not up for consultation or input, nor was it any of Becca's business.

Through prayer and pondering over the next few days, Becca discovered she'd received three beautiful gifts of friendship wrapped in Sarah's bravery, honesty, and vulnerability.

First, Sarah saved their friendship by presenting Becca with an opportunity to make amends. Sarah could have just put Becca at a distance, stopped sharing her life with her friend, drifted away, and let the relationship fade. But instead, Sarah loved Becca enough to fight for their friendship.

Second, even as she hurt, Sarah had the grace to give Becca a chance to learn and grow as a person and to be better for other relationships. It takes a lot of emotional maturity to reach out and say, "We've got to talk." It also takes a certain amount of emotional restraint to listen and reflect on hard feedback. In fact, Becca told me that ten years prior, she would have taken the defensive. Through past mistakes, she knew to take a few days to reflect, empathize, and embrace the chance to become a little more mature as a friend and as an encourager.

As Becca put herself in Sarah's shoes, she discovered that just because someone shares their struggles with you doesn't mean they want you to try to solve the problem or bring it up every time you speak. This revelation helped Becca move forward not just with her friendship with Sarah but with other relationships as well. Becca learned how to listen more than she spoke.

When Becca finally apologized and took responsibility for how she hurt Sarah, Sarah then gave Becca the greatest gift of all: forgiveness.

Y'all, friends are a blessing for sure, but it's hard sometimes. Navigating how people perceive and respond to unsolicited advice can get messy. Becca unwittingly dumped a garbage truckload of stinky diapers on her best friend, and Sarah felt the weight of it. Either Becca's behavior or Sarah's feedback could have ruined the relationship, but instead, they came out of the situation stronger.

I learned two important lessons from their experience. First, we can prevent this kind of situation by clarifying and enforcing our boundaries. Second, if the diapers have already been dealt, we can still turn the trash into treasure.

Boundaries

Perhaps you are also an encourager by heart and always willing to help—but sometimes too willing. One person's idea of help will not look the same for everyone else. Just like we must evaluate the motive and source of unsolicited parenting advice, we must look at our own motive and the recipient before we offer advice.

You may know you are needed when someone shares their struggles, but don't assume you know *what* they need. They may want your advice, but sometimes people just want to vent, share, or ask for prayer.

Why not ask them straight up which friendship hat they need you to wear today? It helps clear the air on what they're really after. Is it time for your clown hat, so you can tickle their funny bone? Or maybe dust off that wise old mentor's hat to share a nugget or two of hard-earned wisdom?

There might be a call for your construction gear, complete with a shovel and gloves, because, girl, we're digging into the nitty-gritty. Or is it more a pajama party vibe, where you're all ears—cozy and ready to offer some southern comfort? Perhaps all they're looking for is to let out a little steam. Well, then, just go fetch some cheese and crackers to go with a perfectly fine good whine.

If they ask for your advice, that's one thing, but there's a difference between an assumption and a clear request, and you better make sure you know the difference. Lead with listening in your heart, and listen to how God is telling you to respond.

Here are a few practical questions you can ask to help your friend define their boundaries.

- Are you asking for my advice, or would you rather I just listen so you can vent?
- Do you want me to tell you what I really think is happening here?
- What does help look like for you right now?
- Can I offer you help with something like research, meals, or chores?
- What friend hat do you want me to wear today?

Sometimes, moms hit you with those middle-of-the-night SOS calls, wondering, "Why on earth won't he stop crying? It's 3 a.m.!" And honestly, just tossing out a "Hang in there, you're doing awesome" might not cut it. When you slip on that educator's hat, ready to dish out a bit of wisdom from your own rollercoaster rides, make sure to lay it all out there—the good, the bad, and the ugly of your experience.

Opening up like that isn't everyone's cup of tea, especially for those of us who tend to keep our cards close to our chest. Going through something and then talking about it? That's a whole other ballgame when the memories are still fresh, painful, and oh-so-personal.

But here's the thing—nobody nails it on their first go. We're all out here making it up as we go, stumbling even when we think we've got it all figured out. Share your story when you're good and ready, and when you do, hone in on what might light a little spark of hope or offer a new angle for your friend.

And if they're saying, "I'm good, really," then your role is simple—lend them your ears and lift them up in your prayers when you're on your own time.

Think about a fashion faux pas. If your girlfriend is about to step out in an ensemble that's more "clash" than "cohesive," would you give her a heads-up or let her learn the hard way? Similarly, if you're reaching out for support and your friend comes at you with advice that's way off base, it's okay to gently guide her back on track. Setting boundaries isn't just about saying "No." It's also about guiding others on how best to support you.

Getting back to the two friends—Sarah had created her boundaries. As Becca overstepped, Sarah considered the source, knowing that Becca acted out of love. Sarah thought she could manage it, but when she sat in it for a while, she realized she had to do something. Sarah couldn't pretend she was okay with Becca's behavior, nor could she parent to Becca's implied expectations.

The only way to preserve both the friendship and her own authenticity was to reinforce her boundaries. In doing so, Sarah not only gave Becca the gifts of friendship and forgiveness, but she also remained in God's plan for her to parent her own children.

Why would you go through the whole vulnerable process of defining your core beliefs, building your social bedrock, filtering the motive and the source, and setting your boundaries, only to allow a caring friend to unknowingly overstep those boundaries? Once you set your boundaries, actively maintaining them is a continuous journey.

Clean Up the Mess

Let's revisit Becca and Sarah's story, but this time through the lens of Scripture, to discover the best way to resolve hurt and conflict caused by unsolicited parenting advice.

Before Sarah reached out to Becca, she took a moment to pray, seeking a bit of that heavenly advice to guide her through the choppy waters ahead. Her actions mirrored the teachings of the Bible, showcasing a moment where divine wisdom helps smooth over human squabbles. Through prayer, Sarah found the grace to approach Becca not with a storm brewing but with a heart wide open, turning a potential dust-up into a testament to the strength of their friendship.

Jesus taught us, as seen in Matthew 18:15, to gently confront those who've wronged us, promising that in their listening, a friendship is deepened. This teaching is a two-way street—it's not just about airing out our grievances but also about giving room for the other to respond with grace.

The Good Book doesn't tell us to stand our ground and holler back our justifications. Instead, it teaches us the grace of listening and the power of understanding.

For those feeling the weight of a friend's grievances, it's a call to hush up and listen deeply, not just to answer back. The courage it takes for someone to share their hurt is a true nod to the trust and respect they hold for you. As you listen, think about how you might've unintentionally played a part in their pain. An apology doesn't just acknowledge the hurt; it honors the friendship and the bravery it took for them to speak their truth.

Luke 17:3 gives us a road map for behavior and forgiveness. "Pay attention to yourselves! If your brother sins, rebuke him, and if he repents, forgive him." The word "rebuke" might sound a bit harsh, but here, it's about sharing your hurt in hopes of mutual understanding, all wrapped up in respect and honor. True repentance isn't just about saying you're sorry—it's about real change and positive growth. Becca's journey of receiving feedback reminds us of the power of friendship and the willingness to grow from tough conversations.

Here's how the Good Lord lays it out for us:

- Act with intention, sprinkled with kindness.
- Share your feelings with a gentle heart.
- Listen not just to reply but to understand.
- Step into their boots and see through their eyes, then apologize.
- Commit to a better path forward.

The trail doesn't end without the crucial step of forgiveness. Forgiveness frees not just the forgiven but the forgiver, allowing both to stride past old hurts. It's about letting go of bitterness so it doesn't sour your spirit.

This journey from a hard talk to full-hearted forgiveness isn't just about fixing friendships; it's a spiritual walk that brings us closer to how God wants us to live with one another. It's about transforming our relationships and ourselves, fostering a community where love, understanding, and grace flourish under the big open sky.

It's a sad truth, y'all, but sometimes we just don't know how to handle the hurts that life tosses our way. Resolution becomes as rare as hens' teeth because, let's face it, nobody's keen on stirring up conflict. We'd rather just shove those troubles under the rug and pretend they're not there, even if we keep tripping over the bumps they make.

The way you handle these moments really lays the groundwork for what comes next in your relationships. Are you gonna hold on to that hurt, stew in it, and let it define you? Sarah could've kept on guessing at Becca's true thoughts. Before long, her trust in Becca might have worn thin as a dollar store dishrag, eventually tearing their friendship apart. Sarah might start building walls around her heart, answering fewer texts, letting calls go to voicemail, and eventually shutting Becca out of her life for good. And Becca? She'd end up lost and hurt, feeling ditched by someone she valued, maybe even gun-shy about opening up to someone new.

Or suppose Sarah spoke her mind, but Becca snapped back with, "Why are you so upset? I was just trying to help. You don't know what you're talking about, so forget you." Reacting with anger or dismissiveness is just like wallowing in self-pity—it's not the grown-up way to handle things.

Just picture this: Every family reunion or get-together with friends has a big ol' invisible guest named "Bitter Resentment." It's like this uninvited critter just sits right there in the middle of everything, making a fine mess of our feelings, turning every gathering into a patchwork of frayed nerves.

Now, what if all our friendships were like that? I reckon we'd be in a real pickle, that's for sure. Smoothing things over takes a heap of grown-up behavior from everyone involved. It's normal to feel all riled up or second-guess what you thought was true. But if you see that feedback as a gift—a real opportunity to look in the mirror, figure out where you stand, and ask for forgiveness—then, girl, you're on your way to mending fences and keeping those friendships golden.

Each relationship in our lives is like a divine assignment—a chance to stretch and grow, provided by the Good Lord Himself. It ain't easy, but I tell you, a true-blue friend is worth more than gold. The Bible lays out simple and clear how to handle offenses, and following those steps is the only way you can clear the air and keep your relationships hearty and strong.

Friendship is a lot like a diamond—full of different facets, each one catching the light in its own way. Sometimes, you might find yourself smack dab in the middle of a volcanic blow-up, with tears streaming down like a spring shower and words whipping around like a tornado tearing through a barn. But, just like a diamond that gets its sparkle from being cut and polished, the true beauty of friendship shines through all that pressure and rough handling.

The real treasure in all of this is the growth and learning—if we let it happen. That's why it's important to have a growth mindset, to stay open to life's ups and downs, to let things unfold, and to dig deep into what we don't yet understand. Every challenge we face is another chance for the Good Lord to use us, to help us fulfill our purpose, and to make a positive dent in someone else's day.

My daughter recently kicked off a new sport. God bless her, she really dug in her heels that first competition but came home with her spirit dragging the ground. I wrapped an arm around her and said, "Darlin', medals sure do sparkle, but the real prize, the one that lasts, is growing a mindset that doesn't quit." It isn't about never feeling down about a loss or stumbling over a setback. That sting? It's part of what nudges us forward, keeping us showing up day after day with grit.

Not caring a lick could just mean you're getting too comfortable where you're at. While those trophies and medals sure make the mantle pretty, it's the relationships you build, the persistence you hammer out, and the resilience you weave into your being that'll stand by you for the long haul.

Get Out of Your Comfort Zone

Joining a minority ethnic awareness group has been one of the richest experiences of my life. Here, folks from the community open up their world to outsiders like me, letting us sit in, listen, and soak in their culture. Most of the time, I'm all ears, just taking it all in as members share the highs and lows they face living in America today.

They've opened their doors wide, letting me get a real taste of life from a perspective that's not the majority. And what a gift that is—to be invited to understand, engage, ask questions, and learn way beyond the bounds of my own familiar corners. I've always just known life through my own lens, but this group has broadened my view, helping me see and value the rich tapestry of cultural differences.

Their experiences and their views—they're just as real and true as my own. So, I've learned to step back, really listen, and try my best to see the world through the eyes of others. It's a privilege, really, to be welcomed into such a personal, sacred space, and I'm grateful for the openness and vulnerability shown.

I've come to understand that my advice doesn't always jive with the unique context or culture of others. This doesn't mean I toss my own views aside; instead, it deepens my appreciation for the wide variety of human experience that stretches well beyond my own backyard.

By stepping right into their world, I've knitted together wonderful friendships with folks I'd likely never have met if I hadn't been willing to step out of my comfort zone and ask those probing questions. It's about keeping your heart open and letting love lead the way. I encourage you to brave those uncomfortable spots, immerse yourself in new experiences, and meet people who push you to grow and see the world differently.

Now, that can be a bit daunting, can't it? Because it confronts us with those parts of ourselves we might rather not face—our shortcomings, our unknown fears, and all those rough edges we've got to smooth out. It takes a heap of courage to grow, and staying teachable is what sets you apart. My mom used to recount tales of a childhood acquaintance who tried to dampen her curiosity, snapping, "You're so dumb. Why do you ask so many questions? Why do you even care?" Turns out, they didn't know the answers themselves. They just didn't want to look foolish, so they tried to hush her curiosity instead.

When you're rooted in a growth mindset, some parts of your core and your foundation stay solid as a rock, while other bits might just shift and change. As you evolve, so do your relationships. This means your values and boundaries might need a little adjusting, and you'll have to stand firm with those who might not see eye to eye with you. Expect some pushback, and be prepared that some folks might not make the journey with you.

Understand not everyone's gonna cheer you on, and there might be some heartache along the way. While it's tough for some to adapt as you change, nobody should expect you to be the same person you were a couple of decades ago. You're bound to outgrow some folks, just as they might outgrow you. That's just part of life's ebb and flow. Don't hang on to their negativity. Don't stick around in places where you no longer fit or where folks aren't lifting you up to be your best self.

Learning sure does ask for a bit of sacrifice because to step forward, sometimes you have to leave something behind. But let me tell you, there's no greater blessing than seeing God use the tears you shed yesterday to ease someone else's pain today. Embracing a growth mindset is about having the guts and the gumption to admit you're still on the learning curve, living true enough to know there's always room to grow.

Not everyone's got the nerve to let themselves be taught a new lesson. You've gotta do more than just tolerate failure; you need to welcome it with open arms if you're aiming to grow and get over those hurdles. It's a daunting spot to stand, admitting you don't have all the answers or showing a soft spot.

If you don't muster the courage to step out of that cozy little comfort zone and stretch a bit, you might just find yourself stuck in the same old spot. Growth sprouts up when you're out there making blunders and letting life teach you the tough lessons. You need to be ready to learn the hard way if you're aiming to fulfill your God-given potential as a momma and to truly live out His plan for your life.

I've come to understand why they say we learn things "the hard way." Nobody's itching to walk through tough times, but that's often how we find a little more growth. In those deep, dark moments, it's a comfort knowing God's right there with us. He's the beacon that not only gets us through but leaves us shining a touch brighter on the other side. And the beauty of it? It doesn't end with us.

Sometimes, the trials we face are meant to mold us, and other times, they're meant to help someone else. Isn't it just like the Good Lord to make sure nothing goes to waste? There's this powerful truth in 2 Corinthians 1:4 about how God comforts us so we can turn around and be a comfort to others. So, if you've navigated the tricky waters of parenting a child with special needs, maybe you're the beacon for another momma just starting down that path. By sharing the lessons and the light you've gained, you help push back the darkness, lighting up the way for others to follow.

Max Lucado sure penned a heart-tugger with *Hermie: A Common Caterpillar*. It's a tale about the plain-Jane troubles that touch our hearts and souls. Hermie didn't see anything special about himself, lacking the fancy spots or stripes the other caterpillars had. One day, Hermie and his buddy Wormie got to wondering why the Good Lord made them so plain, so they up and asked Him. Well, God showed them that each critter is unique and carved out for a special purpose. He's got a plan, and in His eyes, everyone's a stunner in their own way.

It turns out Hermie and Wormie blossom into stunning butterflies, fluttering off to new adventures. And because they started off as plain old caterpillars, they cherished their new world a whole heap more. They saw blessings in ways they never could have if they hadn't crawled around on their belly first.[5]

Here's a curious nugget about caterpillars—help them out of their cocoon too early, and their wings won't toughen up enough for flying. They'll falter and fade right where they land. The wings, which are the most breathtaking part of the butterfly, have to fight through the struggle to get strong and to discover their calling. That's the heart of the struggle, right there. It's about gaining strength, growing into the soul you're meant to be, and catching your own glimpse of your true self. We soldier on, trusting the Almighty to guide us, believing that there's worth woven through our hardships. And we face this cycle over and over, all our days.

As a parent, if you let others dictate every step of your parenting journey, you'll miss out on the beauty of it all, and you might just miss watching your kids soar. Your dear friends can't do the hard work of breaking out of your cocoon for you; they can't shoulder the struggles of parenting or shield you from them. That's on you to tackle.

You may have heard the phrase, "God doesn't call the equipped; He equips the called." You won't find those exact words in the Bible, but Scripture does tell us He will "equip his people for works of service, so that the body of Christ may be built up" (Ephesians 4:12). He's by your side, helping you along the way. And when we find joy in what pleases Him, we're blessed with abundant opportunities to love and serve Him and our fellow folks. We each have a calling—that spark, that desire He's planted deep within our hearts.

As a momma, your God-given calling is to love and nurture your own little ones, each specially crafted with their own quirks and cuddles. But remember, just as God didn't hand me the playbook for your kiddos, He didn't craft you for mine, either. We're here to bolster one another, sure, but you can't parent by someone else's playbook—not without losing a bit of joy along the way. You just can't cherish my children with the same fervor as you cherish your own.

We all make a mark in this world through the tasks God lays out for us. Sometimes, our paths merge for a spell before diverging once again. Through it all, we must stay true to our own light—the divine purpose God has nestled in our hearts. Even through the darkest times, that glimmer of hope propels us forward. In the pitch dark, that's when God's light pierces through the shadows. He's right there in the thick of it, turning gears and paving ways.

The loves of your life—be it your children, your career, or a cause close to your heart—God equipped you uniquely for them. Don't get caught up trying to beam someone else's light; you might just end up scorched or lost. When the world tries to snuff out your sparkle, keep your own flame dancing. Embrace your calling—that special something God stirred within you. Raise it high, stretch it to the skies, and declare to all of creation, "Behold what the Lord has empowered me to do! Witness His handiwork!" Know that these gifts are God's vote of confidence in you—you're here to make waves.

It's tough, no doubt about it, but imagine how much sadder life would be if you never grew, never nudged past those old fences. Think of all the wonders you'd miss if you just huddled in your cozy cocoon, never wrestling your way out. You'd be stuck in the same old sorrows, spinning your wheels on the forgiveness track but never really gaining ground.

So, here's the big question: "What am I willing to lose?" Are you okay with losing your peace, your true self, your grit, or even a treasured friendship just because you're scared to stretch and grow? If you can't stand up and admit that maybe, just maybe, your perspective isn't the only one, if you don't have the gumption to learn from your own stumbles and missteps, well then, I guess I'll have to tip my hat and leave you to pasture with the rest of the stubborn mules grazing in the meadow. Seriously, girl!

REFLECTIONS

Balaam's Donkey

Scripture Reading: Numbers 22

Do you recall a time when you went against the grain of wisdom and discernment and made a decision that ultimately was the wrong choice? Did you recognize the warning signs prior? Did you choose to ignore them? Sadly, I have. Thank the Lord for His goodness, mercy, and forgiveness. Truly.

Why repeat a mistake when you can learn from it the first go-around? It's a question worth mulling over, especially when the Bible offers vivid examples of how straying from God's path can lead us into unnecessary trouble. Consider the story of Balaam and his donkey from Numbers 22.

Here's a summary of the verses:

Balaam's Journey Begins: Balaam, at the urging of the Moabite princes, sets out with his donkey to meet with Balak despite God's initial resistance.

Divine Obstruction: God's anger is kindled because Balaam went, and He sends an angel to obstruct Balaam's path as a form of divine intervention.

The Donkey Sees the Angel: Balaam's donkey sees the angel of the Lord standing in the road with a drawn sword, causing the donkey to turn off the road. Balaam, unable to see the angel, beats the donkey to get it back on track.

The Donkey's Reaction: As the journey continues, the angel moves to a place where the path narrows, blocked by walls on both sides. The donkey, seeing the angel again, presses against the wall, crushing Balaam's foot, which prompts another beating.

The Donkey Speaks: After being beaten a third time for kneeling down and refusing to move due to the angel's presence, the donkey is miraculously given the ability to speak and questions Balaam's treatment of her.

Balaam's Realization: God then opens Balaam's eyes, and he sees the angel of the Lord standing in the road with the drawn sword. The angel informs him that the donkey saw the angel and saved Balaam's life by avoiding him, as the angel would have killed Balaam otherwise.

Admission and Submission: Acknowledging his sin for not perceiving God's messenger who blocked his path, Balaam offers to turn back, but the angel tells him to go with the men but only speak the words that God will give him.

God used a donkey to speak truth to Balaam, highlighting his blind pursuit of personal gain, which nearly cost him his divine mission. Balaam's desire for riches blinded him to God's instructions—a stark reminder of where our focus should truly lie.

In our own lives, the allure of worldly approval and success can often distract us. We strive for recognition, for validation, and for a spot in the limelight, convinced that these achievements will confirm our worth. Yet, in this pursuit, we risk losing sight of the unique roles God has crafted for us—roles like motherhood, where the call isn't to be seen but to serve with love and devotion.

Have you found yourself straying from the path God intended for you? Are you leading others astray in your pursuit of personal goals? Remember, it's not about the acclaim or the accolades. As Matthew 6:33 advises, "Seek first the kingdom of God and his righteousness, and all these things will be added unto you." This verse encourages us to prioritize our spiritual commitments over worldly pursuits, assuring that God's provision will follow.

If you sense that you've lost your way, take a moment to pause and reflect. Proverbs 3:5-6 tells us to "Trust in the LORD with all your heart, and do not lean on your own understanding. In all your ways acknowledge him, and he will make straight your paths." This wisdom is crucial in times of confusion or when decisions lead us away from our divine purpose.

It's never too late to recalibrate and return to the basics of your faith. James 4:8 implores us to "Draw near to God, and he will draw near to you. Cleanse your hands, you sinners, and purify your hearts, you double-minded." This passage is a powerful call to abandon double-minded pursuits and wholeheartedly return to the presence of God.

So, don't be too proud to sit down, reevaluate, and embrace the simplicity of following God's lead. Embrace the humility of returning to the basics, of being a mother as God designed, devoted not to societal standards but to the nurturing and loving guidance that shapes lives. In doing so, you align with God's call, leading not just yourself but also guiding others toward His light and truth.

Prayer

Heavenly Father,

Thank You for the lessons woven into both our victories and our mistakes. Help us embrace the truth that learning is a process and that growth often comes wrapped in the messiness of missteps. When we stumble, remind us that Your grace is not only sufficient but abundant, gently lifting us back up and setting our feet on solid ground.

Teach us to be humble in our mistakes, courageous in our apologies, and gracious in both giving and receiving forgiveness. Help us to listen more, judge less, and love deeply, just as You love us. When we find ourselves holding onto hurt or offering advice where it's not needed, give us the wisdom to pause, reflect, and respond with kindness and understanding.

May we carry the gift of growth from every challenge, and may our hearts remain teachable, anchored in Your truth. Thank You for walking with us through every high and low, shaping us into who You've called us to be.

In Jesus' name,

Amen.

Small Group Discussion Questions

1. The story of Becca and Sarah highlights the impact of intentions versus perceptions in friendships. Have you ever had a misunderstanding with a friend over parenting advice? How did you resolve it?

2. Sarah needed a friend to believe in her rather than fix her problems. Discuss a time when you needed similar support. How did it feel to receive the type of support you actually needed?

3. Reflect on the metaphor of the Old Maid card game from the beginning of the chapter. How does this game compare to the way advice is given and received in real life?

4. The chapter emphasizes the importance of listening and validating feelings over fixing problems. How can we apply this principle in our daily interactions with friends and family?

5. Becca learned a valuable lesson about boundaries through her experience with Sarah. Discuss the importance of boundaries in your own relationships. How do you establish and maintain them?

6. Forgiveness and understanding are central themes in the resolution of Becca and Sarah's conflict. Share an experience where forgiveness played a key role in healing a relationship. What did you learn from that experience?

Self-Care Affirmations

- I am capable of handling the cards life deals me with grace and wisdom.
- I am patient and compassionate, even when facing unsolicited advice.
- I trust my instincts and my ability to make the best decisions for my family.
- I value and respect the boundaries I set for myself and others.
- I embrace the unique challenges of motherhood and find joy in the journey.
- I am resilient and can turn difficult situations into opportunities for growth.
- I seek God's guidance and strength in all aspects of my life.
- I am grateful for the friendships that support and uplift me, even through tough times.

CHAPTER NINE

PRIORITIZING THE NEEDS OF YOUR FAMILY

If there's one thing the whole world shutting its doors taught us, it's that sometimes, you have to stand your ground for the well-being of your family and your own health. No matter your walk in life, keeping your loved ones and yourself healthy and hearty ought to be at the top of your list.

Sure enough, that pandemic was a whopper, but life's full of trials that'll challenge what's important to us. Even when we're solid in our values, backed by a strong support system, and have our boundaries as firm as fence posts, life's not going to stop throwing punches. It's like the world's leaning on our doorbell, hollering, "Ready or not, here I come, and it's not going to be pretty. I'm about to run you down and stretch you out more than you ever thought possible."

Trying to keep family first and focusing on what truly counts when you're pulled every which way can be like trying to lasso the wind. Those needs shift with the seasons of life. So how do we aim true at a target that's always on the move, all while dodging the slings and arrows from beyond our picket fence?

You keep building.

Back when my boys were still young, Cameron and Ethan spent an afternoon playing with building blocks on the living room couch. Cameron, the oldest, was deeply focused, carefully arranging his blocks to build them as high as possible. Meanwhile, Ethan quickly lost interest and started racing around the room with a large toy tractor.

Just as I stepped into the kitchen, I heard a loud crash. Turning around, I saw the blocks scattered all over the couch, with Ethan giving me his best "I'm not sure what happened" look.

While I gently scolded Ethan, I momentarily lost track of Cameron. I turned to find him at the kitchen table, rebuilding his fort with the fallen blocks. This time, he had added larger blocks to the structure, building on a much sturdier surface. With each additional block, he constructed a fort that was even more solid than the previous one.

At the time, it seemed like just another quiet day at home. But reflecting on that moment, I realize it was a valuable life lesson demonstrated by Cameron right in front of me. At his age, I would have created a scene of magnificent proportions with an angry tantrum. I am certain I would have launched myself across the room in a death spiral spin, kicking my sibling to the ground and holding him in an unforgiving headlock.

Aside from the fleeting satisfaction of retaliation, what would the purpose of that be?

The fort was ruined. The blocks were scattered across the couch, and no tantrum would rebuild it. So, instead, Cameron shifted his focus to productivity with impressive results. He chose a more stable foundation to rebuild, using stronger materials and reinforced pillars, and he taught his momma a wonderful lesson about life.

When things fall apart, find a solid foundation to rebuild and make it stronger than before. That's a subtle yet powerful way to handle life's unexpected challenges.

Often, we see being blocked as a setback, a real blow to our spirits. Maybe you stood your ground, and someone didn't like it, so they blocked you. Maybe you refused to bend your beliefs, and now you're cut out from their special moments. It sure can leave you scratching your head, trying to make sense of it all.

But here's a thought—what if being blocked isn't all bad? What if it's just life's way of telling you to pick up the pieces, check the sturdiness of your foundation, and shore up those essential priorities? Instead of dwelling on the negative, grab what remains, ensure your base is solid, and bolster those critical pillars in your life. This approach isn't just about coping; it's about thriving from the ground up, turning what might seem like an end into a brand-new start.

Don't let anyone make you feel you're not up to the task or unworthy of the role God has carved out just for you. Remember, there's no obstacle too big for God to use as a foundation for something greater. Even if life knocks down your blocks time and again, trust that God will always find a way to use them to build up your story!

Every life story has its own rhythm and rules, just like a good country ballad. And in this grand tale of ours, while God is the main writer, He sure does like to let us hold the pen a time or two. We get to decide what we let into our family's story, setting priorities and plotting out our path.

Life's full of hurdles—like a rowdy rodeo—and having a set of rules for your family's boundaries is like having a sturdy fence around your most prized herd. These rules help us face those challenges head-on, providing our kiddos with a blueprint for a well-lived life and creating a legacy as sturdy as an old oak that they can lean on long after we've ridden off into the sunset.

Life Is a Challenge

It seems like life always has something banging on our door, trying to knock down what we've painstakingly built. It's a bit like dancing two steps forward and then stumbling five steps back when life throws a curveball our way.

When we're younger, we tend to look for the silver lining in every rough patch. But as the years roll on and the troubles pile up, finding that deeper meaning can get tougher. We might start feeling a bit worn and a touch cynical as one heartache leads to another, leaving us to wonder, "What's the point of all this?"

Some days are downright tougher than we ever figured they'd be. We might spend days in prayer, searching for answers that seem to play hide and seek. And it's a real challenge to keep marching forward when it feels like you're facing an endless storm. But we can't let the relentless winds of change blow away what we hold dear. Setting up some good, strong boundaries can be our saving grace, helping us decide just what we'll let into our lives and what we'll keep out to protect our family's peace.

Guide Your Family's Boundaries

Just like the Bible lays out God's expectations for us, the boundaries you set are the framework for what's welcome in your home and what isn't. You've crafted these boundaries through thoughtful prayer, shaping them to align with God's plan for you. By choosing which influences to let in and which to keep out, you stay true to who you are and pass on the values that matter most to your kids.

Think of your boundaries as the sturdy pillars holding up the temple of your parenting. They're what give your family life its shape and strength. So take pride in being the keeper of these boundaries, the one who guards your family's heart and home.

Much like the twinge of guilt we feel when we stray from God's commands, it's perfectly natural to experience that same sense when our boundaries are crossed. Embrace these moments as opportunities for learning. Allow yourself the freedom and grace to make mistakes and grow from them. As you firm up your family's boundaries—that critical "No"—you'll also find clarity in your "Yes," crafting a blueprint that guides your children through their own lives.

Your Blueprint for a Life Well-Lived

Each of us holds a blueprint for a life well-lived, tailor-made to our family's deepest needs. To safeguard these, it's crucial to treasure our foundational bedrock and fortify our boundaries against any force that might shake our core. Every family is distinct, built upon unique pillars that steady them through life's quakes.

In my home, we lean on a trio of pillars: balance, peace, and joy, all anchored firmly in a foundation of faith. This sacred blend helps us navigate life's challenges with grace. Whatever your pillars may be, they're there to steady you in the same way.

Each pillar of our needs will face its own storms. When a northerly chill sweeps through, the north pillar might shudder under the blast, but if the rest stand firm, your whole structure holds tight. And if a searing heat from the south threatens, it's best those pillars be as tough as steel, not brittle like plastic. Just like that, our family's needs can be tested from all sides; if my joy seems to waver, my peace is there to steady me.

There's something quite miraculous when, in the middle of it all, we find ourselves at peace from the get-go. It's essential to savor the season we're in, knowing well that our circumstances—and our needs—will inevitably shift. It's through these changes that the deepest lessons are learned. Sometimes, these lessons are not just for us. Our children are always watching, absorbing how we navigate through life's challenges, learning from us even when we least expect it.

And when will these trials end? Well, my friends, the plain truth is they won't—at least not in this lifetime and on this side of heaven. We're bound to face battles as long as we walk this earth, but we can't afford to give up. Our task is to keep our eyes fixed on our path and the legacy we aim to leave. What matters is how we carry ourselves through these trials, teaching those who watch and learn from us how to endure and flourish.

Your Legacy

Cameron, now all grown up, still keeps a steady head even when life throws curveballs his way. Not long ago, when he faced identity theft, my momma instincts kicked in hard—I was all set to go full momma bear on whoever was behind it. But it was Cameron who calmed me down. He reassured me, saying, "Mom, we caught it early. It could have been a whole lot worse. I see where God protected me. Everything is going to be okay."

His words were a gentle reminder to keep my faith strong—not just in his ability to handle life's knocks but in God's presence through it all. I've been blessed to see this resilience as my kids watch how I handle my own battles to maintain peace. Sure, they've seen me falter and seen me crumble under pressures I wish I could erase. But they've also witnessed me rise, turn those troubles over to God, make things right, and embrace the grace to move forward. It strikes me that perhaps our children grasp life's deeper lessons not when they see us at our best but when they watch us wrestle back to peace and joy from the clutches of strife. It's in these struggles, not the easy wins, that they truly learn resilience and faith.

Tim McGraw once sang a tune called "Live Like You Were Dying," which echoes the kind of legacy I aim to leave for my kids. It's the tale of a man who, in the face of dire circumstances, chooses to live life to the fullest.[6] Seeing Cameron mirror this legacy fills my heart with hope. We may not see clear skies in the midst of a storm, but walking in peace with faith that God is watching over His own brings a deep comfort.

Life is made up of a slew of decisions. As grown-ups, we sometimes stray, but boy, it sure is heartwarming when your kids manage to do it a bit better. Cameron, bless his heart, never let anger take the wheel. That really threw me for a loop—in a good way. He held onto peace and gently nudged me to choose my focus wisely.

I've spent a lifetime learning that even if everything else crumbled away, I'd still stand—because my foundation is firm with God at the helm, followed closely by my family and dear friends. These are my non-negotiables—the pillars I refuse to let life's storms shake.

How to Protect Your Family's Needs

How do you safeguard your family's boundaries, lay out the blueprint for your best life, and craft a legacy to lead your kids? It all starts with posing the right questions, recognizing the impact of your words, and clinging to hope.

Asking Questions

Navigating life's trials helps us pinpoint and prioritize our family's needs. When our boundaries are put to the test and our efforts face challenges, we must stand firm for what our family requires. Start by assessing the situation with questions like, "What are my core priorities? How strong are my supports?" We all need to keep our eyes fixed on Jesus, much like Peter did walking on water. The moment he looked away, he started to sink (Matthew 14).

Life is similar to navigating a boat on choppy waters, where shifting winds and swirling waves demand constant balance. That's why it's crucial that our pillars are deeply rooted in our faith foundation.

As you journey through life, there will always be distractions trying to pull you under, challenging you to lose focus. You've put in the effort to define your "Yes," establish your "No," build your bedrock, and fortify your boundaries. Stick to that, and keep steering true.

You've wrestled with determination and prayer to secure all that's precious. Now, hold it close. Rest when the Good Lord allows, stand your ground when you must, and stay true to what's dearest to your heart.

As seasons change, so will the needs of your family. Living day by day, you'll find life itself teaches you what's truly essential. If something threatens to chip away at what your family holds dear, it's time to sit down, ponder, and decide if those needs still hold their place at the top of your list.

If you're out there asking questions and seeking wisdom, you're walking the right path. Remember, you aren't meant to shoulder every burden alone—asking for help is how we're reminded we're part of something bigger.

But, take heed when weighing advice—sift it carefully. Confirm the facts, trust in your own judgment, and keep only what truly fits your family's fabric. Knowing who you are helps you stand firm, making choices that reflect your values and what's best for your family.

Life is no walk in the park, and as you tread through it, you'll find the path often gets rocky. The challenges? They might just get tougher as folks test your limits and try to shake your peace. But hold fast, girl, because God is always ready to lend a hand and haul us out of the mess, day in and day out.

The Power of Words

When life throws its curveballs, it's important to speak your truth—but do it kindly without compromising who you are. If your boundaries need voicing, then, by all means, speak up. Your words are a reflection of your heart, so choose them with the care you'd pick apples at the orchard—looking for the good ones and leaving the bruised ones behind.

I urge you to pause and ponder before you let words fly. Consider the weight they carry and the ripples they create, both around you and inside you. The Good Book tells us our tongue is like a fire and full of deadly poison (James 3). We have to keep it in check, my friend.

And don't just stop at your spoken words—pay attention to your thoughts, too. Ever caught yourself mumbling over a conversation long past? That's because our internal chit-chat shapes a lot of our reality. So plant thoughts that bloom with positivity, gratitude, and faith.

Invest heavily in your emotional and mental well-being. Remember, aside from the Lord and your parents, no one's been with you longer than you've been with yourself. Cultivate a strong bond with your own spirit, trusting your gut and the Good Lord's nudges. Stand firm in your convictions, anchored in divine guidance, and extend the same grace to yourself that you'd offer a friend.

Believe in the transformative power of your words and thoughts—they can sculpt your child's perspective like clay in a potter's hands. Take hold of that responsibility with both hands, and use it to kindle inspiration, elevate spirits, and light up hope in your children's hearts when they're looking for a beacon.

Hope

Now, there's something about the fire that comes up inside us when trouble knocks on our kiddos' doors. It's natural to wanna square up and look that trouble right in the eye—to mark its face so we never let it through our gate again. We want to hold onto that lesson and keep it close like a cell phone, reminding us of what we've learned.

Take that old Christmas classic, *Home Alone*, for instance. There's a momma bear in that story who, upon realizing her cub was left to fend for himself, battles earth and sky to get back to him. With each delay, her worry mounts, but she holds onto a nugget of wisdom—that Christmas is a season sprinkled with everlasting hope.

And that's just it, y'all. Even when it feels like the last ember of hope might flicker out, we've got to dig deep in our faith boots and believe things will mend. We've got to trust that what we're hoping for will come to pass, and the shadows we face today won't darken our doorsteps tomorrow.

In that story, young Kevin does what he has to do to hold down the fort. And that's a lesson for us too. Tough as it might be, we've got to loosen the reins and let our young ones find their own footing. They'll learn, they'll grow, and even though they'll always need their momma, they'll stretch their wings in ways only time can teach. We're there for them, sure as the sunrise, but part of loving is letting them navigate a bit on their own, with hope as their north star.

So let's hang tight to hope, not just as a feel-good thread in a holiday movie but as a real, powerful tool in our everyday lives. It's about believing in the good coming 'round the bend and keeping faith that the trials we face are just setting the stage for stronger days. Hope is that promise that no storm can wash away, a steady hand that guides us and our family through thick and thin.

Hope, that sweet song of the heart, is a whole lot sturdier when we're choosy about our company. The folks we rope in close color our world, impacting how we handle the highs and the rough patches. And it's critical—absolutely essential—to weave time with the Lord into our daily rhythm, fostering faith and spreading encouragement like wildflowers in spring.

Now, here's a bit of sunshine for y'all: Hope is as boundless as the blue sky. Think about it—Earth has its limits, from the depth of the oceans to the stretch of the skies. But hope? It's like the horizon; it's everlasting. When we anchor in the Good Lord's promise that He's working for our benefit, our hope can be as bright and bouncy as a child chasing fireflies at dusk.

This hope we're talking about? It doesn't waver; it's steadfast. Hold tight to it, even when the clouds roll in thick and you can't see the silver linings. My boy Cameron, bless his heart, he caught a glimpse of hope even amidst the trials of identity theft; he saw it as the Lord's shielding hand. And I, too, draw a heap of hope from his strength and resilience.

Admittedly, I've stumbled—more than I care to count—and Cameron, being my oldest, has borne witness to more than his fair share of my missteps. Yet, there's a hope that blooms fresh when I see him echo the good. It tells me something right is springing forth from the soil of those trials.

My children's walk with Jesus plants a never-ending well of hope in my soul. Sure, there are days it feels hidden—tucked away like a secret—and those are the days we dig deep, keeping our prayers fervent and our eyes peeled for those glimmers of light.

But hope isn't just for holding inside; it's for guarding our boundaries, too. With life throwing curveballs and fast pitches, this hope whispers of brighter days ahead. Don't you let the world sketch your portrait when the Almighty's crafted you a masterpiece. Don't conform to others' molds, listening to every wind of advice and losing the essence of who you're meant to be.

It's a fight, all right—a fight to keep the true you in focus, to live spirited and curious. Curiosity—it might've tangled with the cat's nine lives, but what a ride it had before the last sunset. Don't let life stiffen you up, boxed in by others' expectations.

And as sure as the sun sets in the west, there will be those ready to toss shade on your ways and on how you raise your children. But you set up your boundaries like a fortress—strong and sure. Teach your kids to hold that line, too, so they won't have to tread down old, worn paths of regret.

So, keep that hope alive, fuel it each day with prayer and a heart wide open to possibilities. This is how we build a life not just for surviving but for thriving—crafting legacies that echo through generations like a melody that never fades.

A Moment with the Savior

Life sure does keep moving on, just like the currents of a mighty river. Back in Jesus's days, the well in the village wasn't just where you fetched your water; it was where lives intertwined at the break of dawn. The women of the village would gather, sharing the early morning coolness to ease the burden of lugging those heavy, water-filled jugs back to their homes.

Jesus chose such a well as the stage for one of His profound teachings, revealing His true nature to a lone woman—a woman who, burdened by judgment and misunderstood by her own community, chose the scorch of the noonday sun over the sharp tongues of her peers. (I imagine she endured more than her fair share of unsolicited advice.) There, under that unforgiving sun, she found herself face to face with the Savior, a moment just for her, away from the scornful eyes (John 4).

Now, fast forward to our times—society has morphed, norms have shifted, and the way we share and perceive life has taken a new shape. We don't cluster around wells anymore, but oh, how we gather in the digital town squares of Facebook, X, YouTube, Instagram, and TikTok. It's on these platforms where our lives, our ups and downs, our triumphs and missteps, are laid bare for all to see.

It's a curious new world where everyone seems to have a say in how we should live, love, and parent. The chatter that once echoed through village streets now resonates across the globe, magnifying every word we utter and every choice we make. Just like the Samaritan woman, modern moms might find themselves judged not just by a handful of neighbors but by thousands from far corners of the earth.

The influence of a single sentence now stretches far beyond our local community—it can ripple across continents, carried on the digital waves.

This vast exposure can be a double-edged sword, often bringing intense pressure to conform and a constant call for renewal. It's a reminder that while the platforms have changed, the essence of human scrutiny and the need for personal peace remain as relevant as ever.

In navigating these turbulent waters, we're called not just to tread carefully but to find strength in our roots, drawing from the timeless wisdom that transcends generations. Like the woman at the well, we must find our moment in the sun to face our truths, to meet with our Savior in the quiet spaces where we can truly hear His voice.

That's why clinging to hope and faith matters so much, y'all. We gotta lean deep into our relationship with Jesus. That bond? It's our answer, our harbor in any storm. For those of us walking a faith-filled path, Jesus is our cornerstone of peace.

Life, especially as a parent, is brimming with strong emotions. In the thick of raising kids, it's crucial to confront our fears, embrace our true selves, and own our stories. As you journey through life's ups and downs, keep a tight grip on your boundaries. Protect the best parts of who you are, and don't let the dark clouds of negativity pour on your parade.

Every day we show up, we're given a chance to learn, to be present, to be moldable, and to teach. Parenting is a unique voyage, and through your own trials and errors, you gather wisdom like pearls. Don't let yourself fade into the shadows of what others expect of you. Instead, light the way for your kids, showing them how to learn from both your stumbles and your strides.

For the folks just tuning in, if this feels new, you might reckon you've been muting your voice for too long. We can't turn back the clock, but we sure can start making the most of the now. The Good Book talks about redeeming the time—using what we've got left in the best way possible.

Don't dwell on yesterdays filled with regrets or get tangled up in a mess of what-ifs. Decide today what you'll carry forward. Transform those what-ifs into a lesson of growth. What if you had never faced those trials? What if you hadn't reached this point of strength and understanding?

Start today by flipping the script on your challenges. Consider each hard lesson a stepping stone to wisdom. Use your past not as a weight but as a guide. Take bold steps forward, making each day count, with a heart full of hope and eyes set firmly on the path that God has lit up for you.

From this moment on, take it step by step, trusting deeply in God's plan. Remember, you're never walking alone; God is right there with you in every hardship, teaching and guiding you along the way. You're on a journey to discover your true purpose and to learn to love the genuine person you are. You've still got a whole lot of living to do, so start embracing life to its fullest, authentically and wholeheartedly.

Keep on seeking hope, even when the road gets rocky. Those challenges and setbacks? They're just stepping stones, paving your way to a brighter, more hopeful future. Hold on to your faith and keep that hope alive, a bright flame flickering in the darkness.

You're not treading this path solo. Many moms out there feel just like you, wrestling with who they've become because of choices they've made along the way. If that's where you find yourself today, take heart—there's nothing in your life that God can't transform for good. Often, it's those very experiences we wish we could erase that become the building blocks for something greater. In these trials, we discover peace and realize that our toughest lessons and biggest mistakes can truly be our most valuable.

Not a single misstep, not one block out of place, can throw God off course. He's a master builder, using whatever pieces lie scattered around to construct the life He planned for you. You can start moving forward right where you are; there's no need to wait for a better place or time. God didn't create you to just absorb whatever comes your way; He called you to a life filled with love, though it may come with its fair share of trials.

Trust in His promises. You will overcome every challenge, no matter how daunting or prolonged. While the journey might mark us with scars of pain, disappointment, or heartache, God has vowed to use every bit of it for our ultimate good. He ensures that with each battle, we emerge not just survivors but victors, richer from the fight and closer to the life He dreams for us.

For me, one of the toughest parts of this momma's journey is knowing that someday, I won't be here to watch over my kids as they navigate this big old world. And it's not just any kids I'm talking about—mine have special needs. Every struggle and every tough break they've faced is all part of getting them ready for the road ahead. Life's tough lessons prep us for even tougher roads, and that's especially true for my little ones. You can't really leave a mark on this world without having been through the wringer yourself a time or two. My kids—bless their hearts—are no different. We're all going to meet our share of rough patches, but how we shield ourselves and our kin makes all the difference.

God's got a hand in all this; you can bet on that. His faithfulness is as sure as the changing of the seasons, so when the worries pile up and I start fretting about the future, I remind myself that He's already got a plan laid out for each of my kids. And it's not just a back-of-the-envelope kind of plan; it's tailor-made, with all those bumps and bruises factored in. It's about trusting that whatever comes our way, God isn't just watching from the sidelines—He's right there with us, guiding, protecting, and turning every challenge into a stepping stone.

So, while the thought of them stepping out into the world on their own one day sure does twist my heart in knots, I take comfort in knowing they're being shaped for their own unique paths. Just like a blacksmith tempers steel with fire, our trials are shaping us—and them—for what lies ahead. We do our part, sure, setting boundaries, teaching right from wrong, and wrapping them up in all the love and prayers we can muster. But, ultimately, we lean on that grand old truth that God's got us all in His mighty hands, and He's weaving every bit of our lives into a tapestry more beautiful than we could ever imagine on our own.

REFLECTIONS

Finding God's Plan in the Pits of Life

Scripture Reading: Genesis 37-50

Joseph's journey, from the pit to the palace, is one of the most powerful stories of God's providence and purpose working through personal hardship. His life, marked by betrayal, injustice, and adversity, mirrors the trials we often face, teaching us that even in our darkest moments, God is weaving a greater story.

Genesis 37:23-24 describes the beginning of Joseph's trials: "So when Joseph came to his brothers, they stripped him of his robe, the robe of many colors that he wore. And they took him and threw him into a pit. The pit was empty; there was no water in it." Here, Joseph was literally thrown into a pit by his own brothers, an act that foreshadowed the many downfalls he would face. Yet, this pit was not the end of Joseph's story—it was just the beginning.

Despite being sold into slavery and later unjustly imprisoned, Joseph never lost faith. **Genesis 39:21** reveals, "But the LORD was with Joseph and showed him his steadfast love and gave him favor in the sight of the keeper of the prison." God's presence was a constant in Joseph's life, turning each setback into a setup for a greater comeback.

Joseph's ability to interpret dreams eventually led him out of prison and to a position of power in Egypt, where he could not only save his family but an entire region from famine. **Genesis 50:20** sums up Joseph's perspective beautifully: "As for you, you meant evil against me, but God meant it for good, to bring it about that many people should be kept alive, as they are today."

Dear mommas, like Joseph, you might sometimes feel like you are in the pits of life. Challenges with raising children, especially those with special needs, can feel overwhelming and unending. You might question the purpose behind the struggles or why the path is so steep. Yet, Joseph's story is a reminder that no hardship is wasted in God's economy.

Every trial you face as a mom is an opportunity to trust that God is at work, crafting a story of victory out of every trial. Whether it's late-night worries, battles over health, or the daily grind that wears you down, remember that God has a plan for you and your children. He is capable of transforming the deepest pits into the highest praises.

James 1:12 promises a blessing for those who endure: "Blessed is the man who remains steadfast under trial, for when he has stood the test he will receive the crown of life, which God has promised to those who love him."

As you navigate through the valleys, keep your eyes on the promises of God. Your faithfulness during tough times teaches your children to rely on God's strength. Your perseverance shapes not just your character but also molds the hearts of those little ones watching you.

No matter how deep the pit, it cannot out-depth the love and plans God has for you and your family. Stand firm in the faith; keep hoping and praying. The same God who elevated Joseph and used his trials for a greater purpose is also at work in your life. Let your legacy be one of unwavering trust in God's perfect plan.

Prayer

Heavenly Father,

Thank You for the sacred gift of family and the lessons You weave into the tapestry of our lives. In the chaos of daily demands and shifting seasons, help us anchor our hearts in You, the firm foundation that never crumbles. Remind us that even when life feels like scattered blocks, You are the master builder, crafting something beautiful from every broken piece.

Give us the courage to set boundaries that protect our family's peace, the wisdom to prioritize what truly matters, and the grace to rebuild when things fall apart. Teach us to lean into hope, not as a fleeting feeling, but as a steady flame fueled by faith in Your promises. When we face trials, help us stand firm, trusting that You're working behind the scenes, even when we can't see the bigger picture.

Lord, bless our homes with peace, our hearts with resilience, and our legacy with faith that echoes through generations. May our lives reflect Your love and light, guiding our children to walk boldly in the purpose You've designed for them.

In Jesus' name,

Amen.

Small Group Discussion Questions:

1. Resilience in Action: Can you share a time when you felt like you were in a "pit" situation? How did you navigate your way through it?

2. Learning from Setbacks: What is one important lesson you've learned from a difficult time that has helped shape your approach to current challenges?

3. Identifying Support Systems: During tough times, who or what proved to be your most reliable support system? How did this support change the outcome of your situation?

4. Perception of Challenges: How does changing your perspective on a difficult situation help manage the stress that comes with it? Can you think of a time when a shift in perspective made a difference for you?

5. Growth and Development: Discuss a moment when a significant challenge led to personal or family growth. What changed after this growth?

6. Influence on Others: How do you think handling hardships well (or not) influences those around us, especially children?

7. Preparation for Future Challenges: What strategies or preparations have you found effective in bracing yourself and your family for unexpected hardships?

8. Maintaining Balance: When faced with challenges, how do you maintain a balance between addressing the issue and ensuring you don't neglect other important areas of your life or family?

Self-Care Affirmations:

- I am equipped to handle life's challenges, and each obstacle is an opportunity to grow stronger.
- I trust in my ability to rise above difficulties and learn valuable lessons from each experience.
- Every day, I choose to focus on what I can control and release the stress of what I cannot.
- I embrace the journey of personal growth and recognize that each step, no matter how small, moves me forward.
- I give myself permission to rest and recharge, knowing that self-care is essential to sustain my strength.
- My challenges do not define me; they refine me, making me more resilient and empathetic.

CHAPTER TEN

THE MANTLE WE LEAVE BEHIND

As we stand on the brink of wrapping up our journey through the pages of this book, it's like we're pausing at the crest of a hill, looking back over the path we've traveled together. Each chapter has been a step, each lesson a footprint leading us here. Now, as we peer into the horizon of what's next, it's time to draw a deep, country-fresh breath and prepare for the next part of our adventure—crafting a future that's as vibrant and filled with warmth as a Tennessee sunset.

The chapters behind us focused on tweaking, turning, and sometimes tearing up the old blueprints that weren't serving us well anymore. We learned to filter through the noise, to shield our core from the gusts of doubt, and to reinforce our spirits with steel-strong faith.

Now, we're at a jumping-off point—a place to leap into creating the atmosphere in our homes where we can truly thrive. This isn't just about surviving the daily grind; it's about flourishing in it. It's about your kids seeing the best, most genuine parts of their mom in action. It's about the joy that bubbles up when you're living true to yourself and leading your little ones by example.

Embracing this vision of the future is essential because it's the beacon that keeps us steering true north, no matter the storms we weather. It's fueled by hope—the kind that's as nourishing as homemade bread—and the wisdom gained from all our triumphs and missteps alike. Knowing we can reach that vision if we just stay the course is what keeps our hands steady and our hearts steadfast, even when the road gets rocky.

So, as we roll up our sleeves and ready ourselves to paint broad, bold strokes on the canvas of tomorrow, let's keep our eyes fixed on that vision. Let's fill our hearts with the kind of hope that doesn't just wish for a sunny day but dances in the rain while it waits. Let's harness the knowledge we've soaked up like the soil after a good, soaking rain, and let's grow a future for our families that's as lush and beautiful as a well-tended garden.

Together, we're not just moving forward; we're moving upward, reaching toward the kind of future that our hearts have been whispering about all along—the kind where love is the foundation, joy is the framework, and peace is the promise sealed over the doorway. Let's step into this next chapter with courage, with laughter, and with an unshakeable belief that the best is yet to come.

Steering Clear of Borrowed Troubles

If there's one thing us mommas know how to do well, it's worry. We can borrow trouble from tomorrow, next week, or ten years down the line with the best of them. But I've learned, often the hard way, that borrowing fear and anxiety from the future does nothing but stir up a hornet's nest right in the middle of our hearts, minds, and homes. It breeds a kind of rebellion and strife that can turn your inner peace into a battlefield, and that's no place to raise a family.

Now, I'm not saying we ought to ignore the bumps down the road—life throws enough surprises our way without us going blind into the night. But there's a powerful shift that happens when we focus our energy on the here and now—on making those small, positive changes and developing habits that bring our family vision to life. It's like planting a garden. You don't throw seeds on the ground thinking about the droughts next summer might bring. You water them daily, and you pull the weeds—you tend to the garden you can touch and feel.

Maintaining this road we're on is tough, no doubt. Sometimes, a little threat, like hollering, "Don't make me pull this car over!" isn't enough to keep the peace. Sometimes, you just gotta pull over. Maybe even swerve off an exit ramp to recalibrate and take a breather, but then you get right back on that road. And sure, sometimes it's with a white-knuckled grip on the wheel, but you stay the course.

Remember, each challenge is just another mile marker passed on the journey God is mapping out for us. He's preparing us, equipping us with every hairpin turn, every unexpected detour, to face whatever lies ahead with a spirit tougher than old boot leather.

So, let's not waste our grit on what-ifs that might never come to pass. Let's pour it into today, into the very real tasks at hand—raising these kids, loving our families, and turning our homes into havens of joy and peace. Because when we do that, we find that the future isn't something to fear—it's something to build, one beautiful, blessed day at a time.

What-Ifs: Taming the Beast of Uncertainty

Now, let's talk about those sneaky what-ifs. They creep up on us faster than a vine on an old garden fence, twisting around our minds and planting seeds of doubt. You see, living in the cycle of what-ifs is like chasing a ghost through a fog—it's exhausting and mostly leads you nowhere good. They're peculiar little creatures that can either open doors to marvelous opportunities or drag us through the mud, leaving us worn out and wary.

When we start playing the what-if game, we might ignite our imaginations with visions of what could be—a future so bright it'd put the midday sun to shame. But more often than not, these musings turn into a kind of mental quicksand, pulling us down into a pit of worry about all that could go wrong. This endless pursuit can suck the joy right out of the present, leaving us drained and disconnected from the real treasures right in front of us.

I've come to realize that these elusive what-ifs can really warp our perspective, making mountains out of molehills and shadows out of sunshine. They bring a kind of emotional, mental, and even physical toll that can ripple through our family life, dampening the future we're so painstakingly trying to build.

Instead of letting what-ifs dictate our path, why not harness them? Turn them from fears into stepping stones. For every worry that pops into your head, challenge it with a positive spin. What if this challenge is actually a doorway to something wonderful? What if, by overcoming this fear, I teach my kids resilience? Transforming our what-ifs from dread to anticipation not only lightens the load but also colors our journey with strokes of optimism and possibility.

It's like preparing for a storm on the horizon; you can either batten down the hatches and hide, or you can learn to dance in the rain and maybe even find joy in the puddles. So, the next time a what-if tries to cloud your vision, tip your hat and invite it to sit a spell. Have a chat with it and see if you can't turn it into an ally instead of an adversary.

Remember, our children are watching. They're learning how to handle uncertainties not just from what we say but from what we do. By showing them how to meet what-ifs with a calm spirit and a prepared mind, we're not just building a future; we're sculpting their character, brick by hopeful brick.

So let's keep our chins up and our spirits high. Let's face those what-ifs with the kind of hearty courage that tells the world—and our families—that we're here to make the best of whatever comes our way. After all, isn't that what turning the pages of our own life stories is all about? We're embracing the plot twists, finding our paths, and walking them with confidence and a little bit of that country grit.

Expanding Horizons Beyond Limitations

Our vision for the future is often clouded by self-imposed limitations. Maybe some of those were put in place over the years by unsolicited advice, unrealistic social media images, or unachievable societal expectations. Yet, what we see is only part of the story—the possibilities are limitless with God. He has planned blessings for us that far exceed our imaginations. By opening our hearts to a future unbounded by our current understanding, we align ourselves with God's expansive plans for our lives, fueled by hope and driven by divine purpose.

Out on the sprawling plains of possibility, our future often appears as a patchwork quilt sewn from the fabrics of today's decisions and tomorrow's dreams. It's easy to feel confined by the visible horizon, constrained by the limits of our imagination and the perceived boundaries of our capabilities. But, dear readers, let's remember one thing: Our sight may be limited, and we may only see part of the path ahead, but the story of our lives is not written within the narrow margins of human expectation. God's vision for us is as boundless as the sky above those plains.

We sometimes forget, in the hustle of daily chores and challenges, that we are not penned in by our past mistakes or present difficulties. Our lives are not scripted by our shortcomings but are an open field under God's great sky, where He invites us to roam freely. The Lord knows the plans He has for us—plans for welfare and not for calamity, to give us a future and a hope (Jeremiah 29:11). These plans are not confined by the limits we place on ourselves. They are not measured in the small increments of our hesitations or fears but in the vast expanses of His grace.

Let's not stifle our futures with our limitations. Just as a farmer doesn't limit his field's yield by the size of his barn, we shouldn't limit our life's potential by the scope of our current vision. God calls us to a future where our possibilities are as plentiful as the stars. If we dare to look beyond our current constraints—if we open our minds and hearts to the divine expanse—what might we find?

Imagine a life where each morning brings a new horizon, where every day holds more promise than the last. This isn't just a fanciful dream; it's the reality God wants for us. It's a life not limited by what we think we can achieve but propelled by what He knows we can do. This future is built on the solid ground of faith and propelled by the potent fuel of hope.

So, open your heart wide, let your dreams soar, and align your journey with God's limitless plan. It's about steering your life with a compass calibrated by faith, not by the faulty gauges of worldly worry or the finite maps drawn by human hands. Embrace a future where your potential is not predefined by your past, nor is your direction dictated by dread. Let your spirit be guided by the promise of God's Word, and your steps be steadied by His unwavering purpose for your life.

In living beyond our limits, we not only fulfill our God-given potential but also set a course that leads to a richer, more rewarding life. This is the path of peace, the road of resilience, the boulevard of blessings where every mile traveled is a step closer to the person God has called us to be.

Schedule Your Mom Meltdowns: Embracing Emotional Realness

Well, my dear readers, if there's one thing I've learned juggling this bustling life of motherhood, it's that sometimes you just have to pencil in your own unraveling. Yes, you heard that right—schedule those "Mom Meltdowns" like they're as important as any PTA meeting or dental appointment because, frankly, they are!

You see, my days are stacked—a mountain range of athletic practices, ballet recitals, school projects, and, oh, don't forget, my own work that often blurs into the evenings. With all this on my plate, feeling a storm brewing in my chest isn't just a maybe; it's a definite. So, I've gotten a tad strategic: I give my best gal pals, my lifeline, a heads-up. "Heads up, ladies, I'm about to blow!" It's kind of our little code. If they're feeling the heat, too, we synchronize our meltdown calendars for a collective release. Ain't nothing like a shared meltdown to deepen those friendships!

But let's be honest, meltdowns don't always come with a warning. Sometimes, they ambush you right in the middle of the grocery aisle, and before you know it, you and the cashier are sharing a teary moment over spilled beans. These episodes—while fodder for the local gossip mill—are also deeply human. They're our not-so-quiet pleas for a breather, a scream into the pillow of life's nonstop demands.

The truth is, we're all doing our best, but even the best of us trip over our superhero capes now and then. I like to think that each meltdown is just another opportunity to show our kids that it's okay to lose your footing—and it's just as okay to gather yourself and stand back up. After the dust settles and the apologies are handed out, what really matters is that the kids see the cleanup too. They see their momma, humbled yet resilient, crafting peace out of chaos, stitching joy back into the fabric of our daily lives.

I've learned it's not about shielding them from our breakdowns. No, it's about letting them witness the beauty of our comebacks. It's about showing them that every storm passes, and what remains is the strength to start anew with a little more wisdom and a lot more grace.

So, while I don't relish the thought of coming undone, I've learned to embrace these meltdowns for what they are: necessary resets, reminders to recalibrate, and opportunities to model real, raw humanity to my children. Each heartfelt apology and tender make-up hug plants seeds of empathy and understanding. We're teaching them that life isn't about avoiding the falls—it's about learning to pick yourself up, dust off your knees, and laugh together in the aftermath.

So yes, go ahead and mark your calendars. Pre-schedule those meltdowns if you must. Just remember, it's not the falling apart that defines us; it's how we piece it all back together. And perhaps, in showing our children our own vulnerabilities, we're giving them the tools to build their resilience, find their peace, and create joy amid the whirlwinds of their future lives.

Modeling Grace and Conflict Resolution

Now, sweet mommas, let's chat about something we often shy away from—grace and conflict resolution. It's the kind of thing that doesn't quite make the family photo album, but boy, does it deserve a spot! It's like knitting a quilt—each stitch might not look like much, but together, they create warmth and comfort that lasts through the chilliest nights.

How we handle mistakes and conflicts within the family sets a lifelong example for our children. They learn resilience not from never seeing us falter but from watching how we address and amend our missteps. By demonstrating humility and the willingness to seek forgiveness, we teach them that conflict is a part of life and how we resolve it can either forge stronger bonds or leave lasting scars.

First off, let's talk about grace. Y'all, grace is that secret ingredient in the recipe of life that turns a mess into a message. It's knowing that even when the pot boils over or when the cookies burn, there's a chance to start again without holding onto the burnt bits. It's about letting go of perfection and embracing the perfectly imperfect moments that make up our lives. Grace is what you give yourself when the day doesn't go as planned and what you offer to others when they fall short too.

And when it comes to conflict, well, it's as natural as the changing seasons. Every family, no matter how picture-perfect they may seem, goes through it. The key isn't to avoid it—that's like trying to stop the leaves from falling in autumn—but to handle it with care and compassion. It's about finding a way to communicate and to express your feelings without laying blame or building walls.

Forgiveness, now that's a powerful act. It's the oil that keeps the engine of our families running smoothly. It doesn't mean forgetting, no sir. It means choosing to move forward—to clear the air so everyone can breathe easier. And compromise—that's its close cousin. It's about meeting in the middle, where everyone feels heard and valued, not just sticking to your guns and missing the chance to see the world through someone else's eyes.

Communication, well, it's the bridge between confusion and clarity. It's sitting down at the kitchen table, maybe over a cup of coffee, and talking things out until the pieces start to fit together again. It's not just about talking, though; it's about listening—really listening—to what's being said beneath the words.

Finding peace in the resolution—that's the sweet reward at the end of the struggle. It's that deep exhale, that release of tension, when you realize you've weathered the storm together and come out stronger on the other side. It's the quiet that comes after making up when the house is full of soft apologies and quieter affirmations of love.

Balance and joy—they're what we aim to reclaim after every little tempest. Because at the end of the day, what we all want is a home filled with laughter and rooms that echo with contentment.

So, as we stitch these lessons into the fabric of our daily living, let's not forget the beauty in the repair. Each apology, each moment of understanding, adds strength and integrity to our family's tapestry. And isn't that what makes life so richly textured and deeply beautiful? The knowledge that we are all here, learning and growing together, bound by threads of forgiveness, buoyed by endless reserves of love.

And remember, wherever you find yourself in the muddle of motherhood or the dance of family life, you're exactly where you're meant to be. Held in grace, surrounded by love, and always, always moving toward peace.

Cultivating Peace through Legacy and Learning

Reflecting on the legacy of knowledge and grace passed down from my parents, especially my mother's insatiable thirst for biblical wisdom, inspires me to leave a similar legacy of lifelong learning and spiritual growth for my children. What I'm talking about here is worlds apart from that unsolicited parenting advice we sort and filter and, let's be honest, toss some of it out with the wind. This is hard-earned, prayer-backed words of wisdom passed down through generations with love. It's about creating a peaceful home where learning and faith go hand in hand, guiding us through every challenge with serenity and hope.

As we saunter a little further down the path of our parenting journey, it's important we ponder the legacy we, ourselves, are hoping to leave behind. Thinking about legacy is like planning a garden. What do you want to take root and grow long after you've left? What values and memories do you hope will flourish in your family's hearts?

My momma, bless her heart, has always had a passion for learning that was as deep as a well. She wasn't just content with sitting still; she was always reaching for a book or dabbling in something new. When computers started popping up everywhere, she didn't shy away. Nope, she dove right in and learned all she could, eventually helping out at my school's computer lab. Her curiosity wasn't just for her own keeping; she spread that love of learning to everyone she met, including me.

And it's that thirst for knowledge that I wanna pass down—this idea that learning isn't just something you do in school. It's a lifelong adventure. Whether it's through books or cooking or even fixing things around the house, every moment is a chance to learn something new, to expand the horizons of your knowing, learning, and growing.

Now, let's talk a bit about those teachable moments—those times when life hands us a lesson in an unexpected package. Maybe it's fixing a leaky faucet that teaches persistence and problem-solving, or maybe it's a conversation with someone from a different background that teaches empathy and understanding. These moments— they're the fibers that strengthen the bonds of family and community.

And what about those times when things don't go quite as planned? Well, that's when we show our kids how to handle setbacks with grace. It's one thing to celebrate successes, but the true measure of character is seen in how we handle the falls. Showing your kids how to pick themselves up, dust off their knees, and keep marching—that's a lesson that'll serve them well beyond their childhood years.

We also need to be mindful of the stories we tell and the memories we share. Every family gathering, every holiday meal, every quiet night spent under the stars—they're all pages in the storybook of our lives. By sharing these stories with our children, we give them a sense of where they came from and a vision of what they can become. It's about rooting them in the rich soil of family history while giving them wings to soar into their own futures.

And let's not forget the importance of laughter and joy. In a world that can sometimes weigh heavy on our shoulders, teaching our kids to find joy in the simple things—to dance in the kitchen, to laugh at the puppies playing, or to find wonder in a sunset—that's giving them tools to build a happy life.

So, as you consider the legacy you're creating, think about what you want to plant in the garden of your family's future. Make it rich with knowledge, resilience, love, and laughter. And remember, just like my momma taught me about the value of being a lifelong learner, your actions and words are planting seeds that will one day bloom beautifully in the hearts of your own children.

But if you're still on the hunt for that flawless parenting formula, it's time to embrace the truth: There's no such thing as a perfect recipe in this wild ride of parenting. Let's not pack our bags with unnecessary burdens like the negativity of unsolicited advice or the messy what-ifs that dirty up our day-to-day. And for heaven's sake, don't lug around fear, hate, heartache, or anxiety about things that haven't happened yet.

What-ifs are notorious for killing dreams and snatching away our imagination. Instead, why not let those dreams soar? God's got a plan bigger than any box we try to put Him in, and He's ready to bless us beyond our wildest imaginations—if we just let Him lead the way. The emotional baggage we carry? It shapes us, sure, but it also shifts and changes as we grow and learn in our parenting journey.

Think about what legacy you want to leave behind. Every mom dreams of her children knowing deep in their bones that they are loved and that everything's going to be okay. That's the kind of truth that sticks with them through thick and thin. So, as we navigate this path, let's shed the unnecessary, embrace the journey, and inspire our kids with the kind of love and assurance that only a parent's heart can offer.

Some folks say becoming a mom isn't a sacrifice because everything you do is chosen out of love. But even when our choices are wrapped in love, they still often mean setting aside our own dreams and desires. Every decision we make as mothers brings its own set of changes and, yes, sacrifices. It's a bittersweet trade-off, where personal wants often take a backseat to what we do for our children.

Now, I'm no Pioneer Woman or Martha Stewart, but come last Christmas, I figured it might be fun to bake cookies with the kiddos.

So, we dusted off the old recipe books, and right there, nestled between the well-thumbed pages, was my husband's Grandma Mary's treasured recipe collection. Lord, bless her; we lost her while the kids were still only knee-high. I wanted the kids to get a taste of her culinary magic—the kind that only she could whip up, with recipes that had our family licking their plates clean for generations.

As we flipped through that gold mine of mouth-watering secrets, we stumbled upon all manner of concoctions—Succotash, Corn Meal Mush, and Crunchy Ham Casserole. We found recipes for Date Pinwheel Cookies, Never Fail Pie Crust, and, bless her soul, Never Fail Meringue. But then, as we delved a bit deeper, we came across a curiosity that tickled my funny bone—two recipes that seemed to square dance with each other right there on the page: one labeled "Great Cookies" and just a few flips away, another dubbed "Even Better Cookies." Now, how on earth does one top "Great"? If they're already great? Go figure!

After a good deal of wondering, it still perplexed me. Why, if you've struck gold with a "Great" cookie recipe, would you turn around and come up with an "Even Better" one? It got me thinking—maybe, just maybe, it isn't about settling for what's good enough. Maybe it's about reaching for the stars, trying to do your best, and pushing the boundaries of your kitchen prowess.

That's sort of like us parents, isn't it? We think we've got the secret sauce, the perfect recipe for raising kids. We think our way'll fit every child in every kind of way. But truth be told, parenting isn't a one-size-fits-all deal. What works for one might not do for another because each kiddo is as different as chalk from cheese.

Take, for instance, my youngest son, who's more of a whirlwind than a gentle breeze. What he needs to keep him on the straight and narrow might be more like wrangling a tornado than following a recipe for sugar cookies. For him, it's about finding that right mix—maybe a pinch of discipline mixed with a heap of love and a dollop of patience, all while keeping your wits about you.

This dance of sorts, where we two-step between what we know and what we're learning, it's like tweaking those recipes. We adjust, we experiment, and sometimes, we end up with something even better than we imagined. And just maybe, that's the secret to cooking up a life well-lived with our kids. Not following the recipe to the letter, but learning when to follow our gut, add a little of this or that, and sometimes, just going with the flow.

It's all about never settling for "good enough" when you can keep improving, keep learning, and keep loving. That's the recipe for a life full of laughter, lessons, and a legacy of love—more precious than the best "Even Better Cookies" you ever did taste.

Finding that perfect parenting recipe is a bit like chasing the perfect cookie recipe—it's an elusive quest, highly dependent on each individual's tastes and preferences. Imagine flipping through a beloved recipe book and stumbling across a flawless cookie recipe, only to discover an even better one a few pages later. It's a clear reminder that there's always room for improvement, always a new technique or a tweak that might just make everything click a little better. Life, much like cooking, is an ongoing experiment where the willingness to adapt and learn can transform good into great.

Legacy

My mother is a woman brimming with stories and wisdom, much like an unwritten book filled with vibrant tales and insights. She could have been a celebrated author, her life a vivid tapestry of narratives spun from her rich imagination. Her enthusiasm for life is infectious, and she instilled in us a profound eagerness to embrace learning and personal growth. Her kindness isn't just reserved for family and friends; she extends it to strangers alike, teaching us the importance of community and neighborliness.

Her legacy is one of inclusivity and compassion, a testament to her encounters with people from diverse backgrounds. From neighbors who had ventured from far-off lands like India and Saudi Arabia to find a new home in the United States, she welcomed everyone. Through her work and personal interactions, she demonstrated the power of making everyone feel valued and cared for, ensuring no one ever felt left out.

Inherited from her, my mission is to ensure that those I meet feel not only included but genuinely appreciated. I strive to make everyone feel better about themselves after they've shared their time with me, ensuring they know their voices are heard and their presence is valued. Just like my mom, I want to leave behind a legacy of kindness and acceptance, a reminder that we all have a place where we belong and are cherished.

I've got memories tucked away like treasured recipes in a well-worn book—like those Christmases spent stringing popcorn on the tree. We'd sneak bites when mom wasn't looking, only to hear her playful scolding about eating the decorations. But as a reward for our "hard work," she'd whip up a batch of caramel popcorn, claiming it was a treat for a job well done. Truth be told, it was her clever way of getting a moment's peace to finish the garland.

On Wednesday nights, watching "Little House on the Prairie" was like a family ritual. With Dad often away traveling for business, he'd keep in sync with us by watching it too, so he could join in our phone chats, buzzing about what Mary and Laura were up to next. Those were more than just TV nights; they were lifelines, threads that kept us connected across the miles.

These are the little rituals that weave the fabric of a family. They're the simple acts that meet not just the emotional or spiritual needs of our kids, but they bind us together in the mundane and the sacred moments of daily life. Mom was the architect of this legacy. She was always there, subtly ensuring every need was met—not just out of duty but from a deep well of love and joy. Yes, there was sacrifice, the kind that's only seen in the quiet after the day is done when the popcorn is swept up, and the children are tucked in bed, dreams sweetened by the scent of caramel.

As we travel this winding road of parenting, it's crucial to remember that each day offers us fresh chances to shape the legacy we'll leave behind. I often reflect on the valuable lessons passed down from my own folks—the subtle wisdom and the heartfelt sacrifices.

Growing up, my dad was a man of few words, but he had a way of turning ordinary moments into life lessons. He'd often take me fishing early in the morning, the mist still clinging to the water, and while we sat in silence waiting for a bite, he'd suddenly share bits of wisdom. "Patience," he'd say, "isn't just waiting. It's what you do while you're waiting." This nugget of wisdom wasn't just about fishing; it was about life—about enduring the quiet moments and understanding that sometimes, the waiting is just as important as the catching. (Yes, it was unsolicited, if you will—but oh so welcomed.)

Mom was equally influential but in a different arena—she was the queen of the holiday gatherings, managing to orchestrate the most chaotic symphonies into harmonious events that still resonate in my memory. She'd direct the kitchen chaos with the precision of a conductor, each dish a note in the larger melody of our family's story. From her, I learned that leadership isn't about commanding; it's about harmonizing and about making sure each voice is heard and every hand feels needed.

These memories aren't just snapshots of a time gone by; they are the building blocks of the family ethos I strive to foster in my own home. They taught me the value of patience, the strength found in silence, and the power of a well-timed word. They showed me that the essence of our legacy isn't crafted in the grand gestures but in the quiet commitments we make and keep daily.

In this digital age, where every moment is captured and shared, it's easy to lose sight of the importance of those unrecorded, behind-the-scenes efforts that truly define our journey as parents. It's the early mornings spent preparing for the day, the late nights checking homework or nursing a fever, and the personal sacrifices that often go unnoticed.

I aim to pass these lessons on to my children—not just through my words but through my actions. I want them to see the beauty in the mundane, the lessons in the silence, and the love in each sacrifice. This is the legacy I hope to leave—a legacy not of perfection but of presence, not of flawless days but of meaningful moments, each carefully woven into the larger tapestry of our family story.

REFLECTIONS

Passing the Mantle: A Mother's Legacy

Scripture Reading: 1 Kings 19:19-21 and 2 Kings 2:9-14

In the quiet moments of life, when the hustle of daily demands slows to a gentle pause, every mother contemplates the legacy she hopes to leave for her children. The biblical story of Elijah passing his mantle to Elisha beautifully illustrates the profound act of passing on leadership and spiritual inheritance. This sacred exchange between the prophet and his successor offers a touching parallel to the influential role a mother plays in shaping and guiding her children.

1 Kings 19:19 tells us that Elijah, following God's instruction, found Elisha plowing in the fields and placed his mantle—a symbol of his prophetic authority—upon him. This act wasn't just a transfer of responsibility; it was an invitation into a life of greater purpose and divine calling. Elisha's response was one of immediate action; he left his former life and followed Elijah, ready to serve and learn under his mentorship.

As moms, you are continually draping your mantles over your children, often in unseen moments. Each lesson you teach, each prayer you whisper, and each tear you wipe away prepares your child to walk their own path of faith and purpose. Just as Elijah prepared Elisha, you are preparing your children, not just for the world they will inherit but for the divine call upon their lives.

Elisha's request in **2 Kings 2:9**, "Let there be a double portion of your spirit on me," reflects a heart eager to not only continue Elijah's work but to expand it. This is the heart's cry of every mother—that her children would receive her teachings, embody her love, and amplify the goodness she has planted in their lives. Your influence as a mother kindles a flame in the hearts of your children, a flame that can burn brighter and reach further than you could have ever imagined.

As Elijah was taken up to heaven, his mantle fell to Elisha, who then picked it up and struck the waters of the Jordan, parting them as Elijah had done. In this act, Elisha demonstrated that the power and spirit of Elijah now rested with him (2 Kings 2:14). Similarly, the moments you share, the wisdom you impart, and the love you give remain with your children. They carry forward your strength and spirit, equipped to face their own Jordans and to strike the waters with the mantles they have inherited.

As a mother, consider the mantle you are crafting each day. What are the core values and strengths you wish to pass on? How can you intentionally wrap your children in the fabric of faith, resilience, and compassion? Like Elisha, they will one day pick up the mantle you have laid upon them. Make it a mantle woven with threads of grace, dyed in the hues of divine love, and tailored by the wisdom of the Spirit.

In your mothering journey, embrace the power of your role. Like Elijah to Elisha, you are more than a bearer of burdens; you are a beacon of legacy. Your life is a testament, and through your love and guidance, your children will learn to navigate their futures, bearing the mantle you've lovingly passed on.

Prayer

Heavenly Father, thank You for the privilege of motherhood and the profound opportunity to influence the next generation. Help me to lay a mantle of faith and love upon my children, one that they can proudly pick up and carry forward. Grant me the wisdom to guide them, the strength to support them, and the grace to let them grow into the calling

You have for their lives. May my legacy be a light to their paths and a beacon of Your love in their lives.

In Jesus' name,

Amen.

Small Group Discussion Questions

1. How do you handle "mom meltdowns," and what steps do you take to recover from them in a way that maintains your role and respect within the family?

2. In what ways do you find balance between meeting your own needs and those of your family? Share strategies that have worked for you.

3. Reflect on the idea of "borrowing trouble from the future." How can you more effectively stay present and avoid the anxiety that comes with the what-ifs of parenting?

4. What are some self-care practices that have significantly impacted your ability to parent effectively? How do you make time for these practices?

5. Discuss the concept of "passing the mantle" from the story of Elijah and Elisha. How can this biblical principle be applied to motherhood and raising the next generation?

6. How do you involve your children in daily routines that are meaningful and that build family bonds? Share examples of activities that have become cherished traditions in your family.

Self-Care Affirmations

- I embrace the unique role I play in shaping my children's future, acknowledging my influence as a gift of love and legacy.
- I grant myself permission to pause, reflect, and rejuvenate, knowing that my well-being is essential to my family's harmony.
- Every day, I choose to weave patience, love, and understanding into the fabric of my family life.
- I am confident in the legacy I'm creating, crafted with moments of kindness, strength, and integrity.
- I allow myself grace in moments of struggle, knowing that every challenge is an opportunity to demonstrate resilience to my children.
- I am deserving of moments of peace and joy, and I actively seek opportunities to nurture my spirit and joy.
- I celebrate each act of self-care as a vital step toward sustained health and happiness, setting a positive example for my family.
- With each breath, I remind myself of my worth and embrace the journey of motherhood with an open heart and a resilient spirit.

CHAPTER 11

EMBRACING THE BEAUTIFUL UNKNOWN

Well, we made it, mommas. Phew! Navigating the murky waters of unsolicited parenting advice is a journey every parent walks. Throughout this book, we've delved into the highs and lows of dealing with well-meaning, yet often misplaced, suggestions from friends, family, and even strangers. One of the most crucial lessons learned is the importance of filtering advice through the lens of your own values and circumstances. Not every piece of advice will fit your family's unique dynamic, and that's okay. It's essential to discern what aligns with your beliefs and parenting style while gracefully letting go of what doesn't resonate.

When faced with unsolicited advice, it's vital to remember that most people genuinely want to help, even if their approach is less than perfect. A key takeaway is the value of patience and empathy in these interactions. Rather than reacting defensively, take a moment to consider the intent behind the advice. Sometimes, listening with an open heart can reveal nuggets of wisdom you might have otherwise dismissed. And when the advice truly doesn't fit, it's perfectly acceptable to politely thank the person and continue on your path, confident in your choices.

One of the most profound lessons is the impact of modeling how to handle unsolicited advice for your children. They observe not only how you interact with others but also how you maintain your boundaries with grace and respect. By showing them that it's possible to stand firm in your decisions while remaining kind and open-hearted, you teach them resilience and confidence in their own judgment. This balance of firmness and empathy is a cornerstone of effective parenting and leaves a lasting legacy for your children to carry into their own future.

Reflecting on the Journey

As we draw close to the final pages of this book, let's take a moment to pause and reflect on the journey we've traveled together. Each chapter has been a step along a path, marked by the footprints of our shared experiences and the lessons we've uncovered. It's much like standing on a hill, looking back over the winding road that brought us here, appreciating every twist and turn that shaped our way.

In Chapter One, we set the stage by exploring the importance of understanding and embracing our roles as mothers. We delved into the essence of trust and faith and how they guide us through the unpredictability of parenting. By grounding ourselves in these principles, we found a solid foundation upon which to build.

Chapter Two took us deeper into the heart of faith, illustrating the importance of prayer and spiritual connection. We learned that through faith, we could navigate the challenges and uncertainties of motherhood with a sense of peace and purpose.

As we moved into Chapter Three, we began to address the external influences and how they shape our parenting journey. We discussed the need to filter through the noise and focus on what truly matters, ensuring that our core values remain intact despite the distractions of the world.

Chapter Four introduced the concept of setting boundaries, emphasizing that saying "No" can be as powerful as saying "Yes." We explored how maintaining these boundaries protects our family's well-being and helps us stay true to our values.

In Chapter Five, we explored the importance of community and connection. We recognized that while our individual journeys are unique, we are not alone. By leaning on each other and sharing our stories, we build a network of support that strengthens us all.

Chapter Six took us into the realm of seeking advice and wisdom. We learned that asking for help is not a sign of weakness but a testament to our commitment to growth and learning. By opening ourselves to the insights of others, we enrich our own journey.

Chapter Seven touched on the deeply sensitive subject of loss and how to seek and give support in times of grief. We discovered that through shared pain and the courage to reach out, we find healing and resilience.

In Chapter Eight, we acknowledged that mistakes are inevitable and learning is a continuous process. We emphasized the importance of grace—both for ourselves and others—as we navigate the complexities of parenting and life.

Chapter Nine highlighted the necessity of prioritizing our family's needs, even amid life's chaos. We discussed practical ways to ensure that our family's well-being remains at the forefront, fostering a nurturing environment where everyone can thrive.

Chapter Ten encouraged us to look ahead with hope and determination. We focused on embracing a vision for the future, steering clear of borrowed troubles, and expanding our horizons beyond self-imposed limitations.

Through each chapter, we've shared stories, insights, and practical advice, weaving a tapestry of wisdom and love. We've laughed, cried, and learned together, finding strength in our shared experiences. This journey has not only been about navigating unsolicited parenting advice and the challenges of motherhood in general but also about growing as individuals and as a community.

As we reflect on the path we've walked, let us carry forward the lessons we've learned. Let us remember that every step, no matter how small, has brought us closer to our true selves and to the mothers we aspire to be. This book may be nearing its end, but our journey continues, filled with endless opportunities for growth, joy, and fulfillment.

Trusting in Divine Guidance

Y'all, let me tell you something about life's winding road: It's full of unexpected turns, detours, and those sneaky potholes that jolt you right when you think you're cruising smoothly. But here's the beauty of it all—we don't travel this road alone. Just as a country road stretches out beneath a big, open sky, our lives unfold under the watchful eye of a loving God. It's His guidance that lights our way, even when the path seems unclear.

Remember that time you found yourself at a crossroads, not knowing which direction to take? Maybe it was choosing a school for your kids, deciding on a career change, or facing a tough family decision. In those moments of uncertainty, it's easy to feel lost, like you're wandering in a dense forest with no compass. But that's when we need to lean in, quiet our minds, and listen for that still, small voice that whispers, "This is the way; walk in it."

I've found that trusting in God's guidance isn't about having a detailed map with every twist and turn clearly marked. No, it's more like holding a lantern that lights just enough of the path ahead to take the next step. It requires faith, the kind that grows deep roots in the rich soil of experience and prayer. And let me tell you, those roots will hold strong even in the fiercest storm.

One of the most powerful lessons I've learned is that God's timing is perfect, even when it doesn't align with our own schedules and plans. We're often in a rush, wanting immediate answers and quick fixes. But God, in His infinite wisdom, sees the bigger picture. He knows that sometimes, we need to wait, to grow, and to prepare for what lies ahead. It's in those seasons of waiting that our faith is stretched and strengthened.

There was a time when I was desperate for answers about my son's health, seeking clarity and a solution that seemed so elusive. I prayed, I researched, and I sought advice from every corner. But it wasn't until I surrendered my fears and anxieties to God, trusting that He had a plan, that I found peace. It was a peace that didn't come from having all the answers but from knowing that God was in control, guiding me through each step of the journey.

So, as you stand at your own crossroads, take heart. Trust that God's got this. He's been with you every step of the way, from the moment you held your child for the first time to the countless nights you've spent in prayer and contemplation. He's seen every tear and heard every whispered hope. And He's preparing a way for you, even now.

Let's embrace the journey with confidence, knowing that we are guided by a loving Creator who knows the path better than we ever could. Let's walk forward with faith, trusting that each step, no matter how small, is part of a grander plan. And let's encourage our children to do the same, teaching them to lean on God's wisdom and to seek His guidance in all things.

As we continue this beautiful, challenging, and unpredictable journey of motherhood, let's hold tight to the truth that we are never alone. God is our constant companion, our steadfast guide, and our source of unending hope. He always has your best intentions at heart, and you can take His advice to the bank every time. Trust in Him, dear friends, and watch as He leads you to places of blessing beyond your wildest dreams.

Embracing the Journey Together

Oh, sweet mommas, we've journeyed through so much together in these pages, haven't we? We've navigated the ups and downs of motherhood. And here we are, nearing the end of our journey together, but let's remember, our story is far from over. This adventure of motherhood, faith, and life is one we get to embrace every single day, side by side.

There's something truly special about knowing we're not alone in this. Just like the fields of wildflowers that blanket the countryside, we're part of a beautiful, vibrant community. Each of us brings our own unique color and fragrance to the tapestry of life, and it's this diversity that makes our journey so rich and rewarding.

Let's take a moment to appreciate the strength we find in each other. When the road gets rough, and we feel like we're carrying the weight of the world on our shoulders, it's often a friend's kind word or a loved one's reassuring hug that helps us keep going. It's in these connections that we find the courage to face our fears, the wisdom to make tough decisions, and the joy to celebrate even the smallest victories.

I remember a time when I was knee-deep in the chaos of raising little ones, feeling utterly overwhelmed and exhausted. One day, a dear friend showed up at my doorstep with a casserole in hand and a heart full of encouragement. She didn't come with solutions or judgments—just a listening ear and a comforting presence. That simple act of love and support was like a lifeline, reminding me that I wasn't alone and that together, we could weather any storm.

And isn't that what we all need sometimes? A reminder that we're in this together. That we're part of a larger story—one that's woven with threads of faith, hope, and love. We may each be on our own unique path, but our journeys intersect in the most beautiful ways, creating a network of support that's stronger than any one of us could be alone.

As we continue to walk this road, let's make a commitment to lift each other up. Let's be the friend who shows up with a casserole, the mom who offers a listening ear, and the neighbor who extends a helping hand. Let's build a community where grace flows freely, where kindness is the norm, and where everyone feels valued and loved.

We also need to embrace the truth that our journey is about progress, not perfection. It's easy to fall into the trap of comparison, especially in this age of social media, where everyone's highlights are on full display. But remember, behind every perfect photo is a real story, filled with challenges and imperfections just like ours. Let's celebrate the real, messy, and beautiful moments that make up our lives, knowing that it's these experiences that shape us and our children.

And speaking of our children, let's cherish the journey we're on with them. Each stage, from the sleepless nights of infancy to the turbulent teenage years, brings its own set of joys and challenges. But through it all, we have the incredible privilege of guiding, nurturing, and loving these precious souls. Let's be present for them, savoring the small moments and celebrating the big milestones. Let's show them what it means to live a life of faith, resilience, and love.

Celebrating Small Victories

Now, if there's one thing I've learned in this grand adventure called motherhood, it's that the little moments often carry the biggest weight. In the hustle and bustle of daily life, it's so easy to overlook the small victories that add up to something truly remarkable. But I'm here to tell you, those tiny triumphs are worth celebrating with all the gusto of a country fair.

You see, life isn't always about the big, flashy achievements. It's about those sweet, everyday moments that knit our hearts together and remind us of the beauty in the ordinary. Like when your toddler finally masters the art of using the potty, or when your teenager unexpectedly offers to help with the dishes without being asked. Those are the moments that make you pause, take a deep breath, and think, "Yes, we're doing all right."

I remember one particular day when my youngest, Ethan, finally managed to tie his shoes all by himself. Now, to the outside world, it might seem like a small feat, but in our house, it was like he had just scaled Mount Everest. We cheered, clapped, and even did a little happy dance right there in the middle of the kitchen. Because, at that moment, we weren't just celebrating tied shoelaces—we were celebrating perseverance, growth, and the sweet satisfaction of a job well done.

These small victories are the heartbeat of our daily lives. They're the threads that weave together the tapestry of our family's story. And when we take the time to acknowledge and celebrate them, we're not just building confidence in our children—we're building a legacy of gratitude and joy.

And what about those quiet moments when we sneak into our children's rooms at night, watching them sleep with the peaceful innocence only children have? The room might be littered with toys and the laundry basket overflowing, but in that hushed stillness, we find a serene victory. It's the calm after the storm, a gentle reminder that amidst the chaos, there is always a moment of peace.

Celebrating these small victories also means giving ourselves a pat on the back. Motherhood isn't for the faint of heart, and sometimes, just getting through the day deserves a round of applause. Did you manage to keep everyone fed, clothed, and relatively happy today? That's a win in my book. Did you find a few minutes to sip your coffee while it was still hot? Go ahead and celebrate that too.

These small celebrations don't have to be grand affairs. Sometimes, it's the simple act of acknowledging them that makes all the difference. A whispered "well done" to yourself, a high-five with your spouse, or a quick text to a friend sharing your tiny triumph can turn an ordinary day into something extraordinary.

One thing I've come to cherish is our family's tradition of sharing "the best part of our day" at dinner each evening. It's a simple practice, but it's become a sacred time where we pause to reflect on the good, no matter how small. Hearing my kids recount their highlights, from acing a test to making a new friend at school, fills my heart with gratitude and joy. It's a gentle reminder that even on the hardest days, there's always something to be thankful for.

And let's not forget the power of gratitude in our own lives. Taking a moment each day to jot down a few things we're thankful for can transform our perspective. It shifts our focus from what's lacking to what's abundant, from the struggles to the blessings. It's like a breath of fresh air for our souls, renewing our strength and filling our hearts with joy.

As we journey forward, let's make a conscious effort to celebrate those small victories with as much enthusiasm as the big ones. Let's teach our children to find joy in the little things, to appreciate the beauty in the mundane, and to cherish the simple moments that make life sweet. Because, at the end of the day, it's these small victories that create the mosaic of a life well-lived.

So here's to the everyday triumphs, the tiny moments of joy, and the quiet victories that fill our hearts with gratitude. Let's celebrate them all, knowing that each one is a stepping stone on the path to a beautiful, fulfilling future. And let's do it together as a community of moms who understand that in the grand tapestry of life, every thread counts.

Embracing the Unscripted Moments

Life, as you know, doesn't always go according to plan. In fact, more often than not, it seems to have a mind of its own. Just when you think you've got everything figured out, something comes along to throw you off balance. And that's okay. It's more than okay—it's part of the journey.

One of the greatest lessons I've learned as a mom is to embrace the unscripted moments, those times when life veers off the carefully charted course and takes us somewhere unexpected. Because, believe it or not, it's in those moments that we often find the sweetest memories, the biggest laughs, and the most profound growth.

Embracing the unscripted moments also means being present and fully engaged with our children. It's about putting down the to-do list, stepping away from the chores, and really immersing ourselves in their world. It's about saying yes to that impromptu dance party in the living room, to the spontaneous baking session that leaves the kitchen a mess, and to the endless questions and curiosities that fuel their young minds.

Children have a way of teaching us the value of spontaneity and the joy of living in the moment. They remind us that life isn't meant to be perfectly scripted but beautifully lived. By embracing these unscripted moments, we show them that it's okay to be flexible, to adapt, and to find joy in the unexpected.

So, the next time life throws you a curveball, take a deep breath and embrace it. Laugh at the mishaps, cherish the surprises, and find the beauty in the detours. Remember, it's often in the unscripted moments that we discover the true essence of life—a life filled with love, laughter, and unforgettable memories.

Let's teach our children to see the value in these moments, to roll with the punches, and to find joy in the journey. Because when we do, we not only enrich their lives but also our own. Life may not always go according to plan, but that's what makes it an adventure worth living.

As we embrace the unscripted moments, we create a home filled with spontaneity, laughter, and a deep sense of connection. And isn't that what life's all about? Sharing these precious moments with those we love, creating memories that will last a lifetime, and finding joy in every twist and turn of the journey. So, here's to the unscripted moments—may we embrace them with open arms and hearts full of gratitude.

The Power of Letting Go

Letting go is a phrase that often comes with a heavy sigh, like it carries the weight of the world. And in many ways, it does. As parents, letting go can mean a host of things—letting go of control, of expectations, of fears, and sometimes, of the tiny hands that once clung to us so tightly. But in the process of letting go, we often find freedom, growth, and the beautiful unfolding of our children's independence.

One of the most poignant moments of letting go for me was the first day of school for each of my kiddos. There's something heart-wrenching yet profoundly satisfying about watching your little one walk into a classroom for the first time, a backpack almost as big as they are, bravely stepping into a world of unknowns. I remember standing at the school gate, fighting back tears and a hundred different worries—would they make friends, would they be scared, would they need me?

But as I watched them disappear into the sea of children, I realized that this was their journey to take. It was time for me to step back and trust that they were ready, that I had prepared them as best as I could, and that they would find their way. Letting go in that moment wasn't just about releasing my grip; it was about embracing their ability to grow and thrive without me hovering nearby.

Letting go isn't just about the big milestones like the first day of school. It's in the everyday moments too—the times when we step back and let our children solve their own problems, make their own mistakes, and learn their own lessons. It's about resisting the urge to swoop in and fix everything and, instead, allowing them to navigate the ups and downs of life with a sense of autonomy.

I remember one particular evening when one of my sons was trying to build a model car. He was frustrated because the pieces wouldn't fit together as easily as he'd hoped. My instinct was to jump in and help him, to show him the right way to do it. But something held me back. I watched as he wrestled with the pieces, his brow furrowed in concentration. Finally, after what felt like an eternity, he figured it out. The look of pride and accomplishment on his face was worth every moment of restraint.

In that moment, I learned that letting go also means giving our children the gift of confidence. By allowing them to face challenges on their own, we help them build resilience and self-reliance. They learn that they are capable, that they can overcome obstacles, and that success often comes from perseverance and hard work.

Of course, letting go isn't always easy. It can be downright terrifying. But it's also necessary. Our children need space to grow, to explore, and to discover who they are without us constantly guiding their every move. They need to know that we trust them, that we believe in their abilities, and that we support them even when they stumble.

Letting go also means letting go of our own expectations and dreams for our children. It's about accepting them for who they are, not who we want them to be. It's about celebrating their unique gifts and talents, even if they're different from our own. It's about allowing them to chart their own path, even if it leads in a direction we hadn't anticipated.

In letting go, we find a new kind of joy—a joy that comes from watching our children become their own people, from seeing them achieve things we never imagined, and from knowing that they are happy and fulfilled in their own right. We discover that our role as parents isn't to mold them into a specific image but to love and support them as they grow into the unique individuals they were meant to be.

So, here's to letting go. To stepping back and trusting that our children have what it takes to navigate the world. To embracing the uncertainty and finding peace in knowing that we've done our best. To celebrating their independence and cheering them on as they chase their dreams. Letting go isn't about losing control; it's about gaining a deeper connection with our children and a greater appreciation for the incredible people they are becoming.

As we journey through this process of letting go, let's remember that it's not about perfection. It's about progress. It's about learning and growing alongside our children. And it's about finding the courage to let them fly, knowing that they'll always find their way back home. Because at the end of the day, letting go is an act of love—a love that trusts, that believes, and that lets go so that it can hold on to what truly matters.

Embracing the Unexpected

Life has a way of throwing us curveballs when we least expect it. Just when we think we have everything figured out, something unexpected comes along and changes our course. Embracing the unexpected can be challenging, but it's also an essential part of our journey as parents and individuals. It's about finding grace in the chaos and discovering the beauty in the unforeseen moments.

One summer, our family planned a long-awaited vacation to the beach. We had everything meticulously planned out—our bags were packed, the route was mapped, and we had a list of activities to enjoy. But as we set off, the car broke down halfway to our destination. It was scorching hot, and we were stuck on the side of the road, miles from the nearest town. My initial reaction was frustration and disappointment. All our plans seemed to crumble in an instant.

But as we waited for the tow truck, something beautiful happened. We spread out a blanket on the grass by the roadside and had an impromptu picnic. The boys explored the nearby field, chasing butterflies and laughing. We shared stories, played games, and soaked in the unexpected adventure. That unplanned picnic became one of the most memorable parts of our trip. It taught me that sometimes, the best moments are the ones we don't plan for.

Embracing the unexpected means being flexible and open to change. It means seeing interruptions not as inconveniences but as opportunities for growth and connection. It's about finding joy in the detours and being willing to let go of our plans to make room for new experiences.

When Ethan was diagnosed with a learning disability, it felt like the ground had shifted beneath our feet. We had to adjust our expectations and find new ways to support his learning. It wasn't easy, and there were moments of doubt and frustration. But through this journey, we discovered strengths and talents in Ethan that we might never have seen otherwise. We learned to celebrate his unique way of seeing the world and to appreciate the resilience and determination he showed in overcoming challenges.

Embracing the unexpected also means being open to new opportunities. Sometimes, life's detours lead us to places we never imagined but end up being exactly where we need to be. It's about trusting that there's a greater plan at work, even when we can't see the whole picture.

When I finally decided to pursue the music career I had always dreamed of but never had the courage to pursue, it was a leap of faith, and it came with its own set of challenges. But it also brought immense fulfillment and growth. It reminded me that sometimes, what seems like a setback is actually a setup for something greater.

As parents, we often strive to create a sense of stability and predictability for our children. But it's equally important to teach them to embrace the unexpected, to be adaptable and resilient in the face of change. By modeling this mindset, we equip them with the tools to navigate life's uncertainties with grace and confidence.

So, let's embrace the unexpected with open hearts and open minds. Let's find beauty in the detours and joy in the surprises. Let's teach our children that it's okay to change course, to dream new dreams, and to find adventure in the unplanned moments. Because in the end, it's the unexpected twists and turns that make our journey rich and full of life.

Celebrate the Small Moments: Life is made up of countless small moments that weave together to create a rich tapestry. Celebrate the simple joys, the quiet victories, and the everyday blessings. These moments are the heartbeats of our journey.

Seek Balance: In the hustle and bustle of daily life, strive to find a balance that nurtures your soul and supports your family. Make time for rest, for play, and for the things that bring you joy. Balance isn't about perfection; it's about finding harmony in the midst of chaos.

Prioritize Connection: Relationships are the foundation of a meaningful life. Prioritize time with your loved ones, invest in deep and meaningful connections, and cherish the bonds that hold your family together. In the end, it's the people we love that matter most.

Embrace Flexibility: Life rarely goes according to plan, and that's okay. Embrace flexibility and be open to change. Trust that even when things don't go as expected, there's beauty and growth to be found in the unexpected.

Let Go and Trust: Letting go of control can be one of the hardest lessons to learn, but it's also one of the most liberating. Trust in yourself, trust in your children, and trust in the journey. Know that you've equipped them with the tools they need to navigate the world.

Keep Learning and Growing: Never stop learning. Be curious, be open, and be willing to grow. Life is a continuous journey of discovery, and there's always something new to learn.

Live with Hope and Joy: Cultivate a spirit of hope and joy. Let your faith guide you, and let your heart be filled with gratitude. Find joy in the journey, and let hope light your way, even in the darkest of times.

Embracing the Journey Forward

Y'all, we've been through quite the journey together, haven't we? We've laughed, we've cried, and we've shared so many precious moments. As we bring this journey to a close, let's remember that our path as parents is never about reaching perfection. It's about embracing every twist and turn with grace and a smile, especially when it comes to handling unsolicited parenting advice.

Each piece of advice, each heartfelt story, has woven a tapestry of resilience, love, and unending faith. We've learned to filter through the noise, taking to heart what aligns with our values and letting go of what doesn't. We've discovered the importance of patience and empathy, even when advice is offered with less-than-perfect delivery. And we've realized that teaching our children how to handle unsolicited advice with grace and confidence is one of the greatest gifts we can give them.

So here's to us, the mommas who face each day with courage and a touch of humor, who lean on each other and trust in God's guiding hand. As we move forward, let's cherish the small victories, celebrate the unexpected moments, and hold tight to the belief that we are exactly where we're meant to be. Together, we are creating a legacy of love, faith, and joy that will light the way for our children and their children after them.

So keep your hearts open and your spirits high, embrace the advice that lifts you up, and gracefully let go of what doesn't. Let's embrace this beautiful journey forward, one step at a time.

ENDNOTES

<u>Chapter One</u>

[1] Robert Rich, Jr., MD, familydoctor.org, "Mental Health: Keeping Your Emotional Health," accessed September 7, 2024, https://familydoctor.org/mental-health-keeping-your-emotional-health/.

[2] CDC.gov, "About Mental Health," accessed September 7, 2024, https://www.cdc.gov/mentalhealth/learn/index.htm.

<u>Chapter Two</u>

[3] Stephen Covey, *The Seven Habits of Highly Effective People* (Mango, 2022), Part One, Kindle.

<u>Chapter Seven</u>

[4] David Hernandez, How to Know You Are in God's Will - 3 IMPORTANT Signs (2022),https://www.youtube.com/watch?v=jOGUjCsRLlU&lc=UgyjCXHJJSCi7x9UbN14AaABAg

<u>Chapter Eight</u>

[5] Max Lucado, *Hermie: A Common Caterpillar* (Thomas Nelson, 2002), board book.

<u>Chapter Nine</u>

[6] Tim McGraw, "Live Like You Were Dying," track 5 on *Live Like You Were Dying*, Curb Records, 2004.

ANDREA HOLMAN is the kind of woman who can make you laugh, think, and feel like you've known her forever-all in the same breath. A light-hearted yet deeply inspirational author, speaker, singer, and entertainer, Andrea has a way of meeting people right where they are, wrapping them in a big ol' hug of encouragement, and reminding them of the joy in every journey. Whether she's behind a microphone, on a stage, or putting pen to paper, one thing is certain: she leads with her heart, her faith, and a good dose of quick wit.

Born and raised with deep Southern roots, Andrea's East Tennessee influence shines through in everything she does. She tells it like it is, sprinkles in a little sass, and keeps it real-because life's too short for anything less. Her humor is infectious, her stories are relatable, and her message is clear: faith, family, and finding joy in the everyday moments matter most. She's married to her best friend, Luke, who has been her rock, her partner in crime, and occasionally the target of her best punchlines. Together, they've built a beautiful (and often hilariously chaotic) life with their four children in Cincinnati, Ohio-a city she now calls home but where she still proudly waves her Southern banner high.

Whether she's singing a heartfelt song, sharing a powerful message, or making an audience double over in laughter, Andrea's goal remains the same—to inspire, uplift, and be a friend to all. Because at the end of the day, she believes we're all in this together, and a little faith, a little humor, and a whole lot of love can go a long way.

www.ingramcontent.com/pod-product-compliance
Lightning Source LLC
Chambersburg PA
CBHW030231100526
44583CB00013BA/714